STATISTICS 3/4

Walker Maths Essentials: Statistics 3/4
1st Edition
Charlotte Walker
Victoria Walker

Cover and text design: Cheryl Smith, Macarn Design
Production controller: Siew Han Ong

Acknowledgements
Cover photo courtesy of Shutterstock

The authors wish to thank past and present colleagues who have generously shared their expertise and ideas.

For product information and technology assistance,
in Australia call **1300 790 853**;
in New Zealand call **0800 449 725**

For permission to use material from this text or product, please email **aust.permissions@cengage.com**

National Library of New Zealand Cataloguing-in-Publication Data
A catalogue record for this book is available from the National Library of New Zealand

978 01 7044725 6

Cengage Learning Australia
Level 5, 80 Dorcas Street
Southbank VIC 3006 Australia

Cengage Learning New Zealand
For learning solutions, visit **cengage.co.nz**

Printed in China by 1010 Printing International Limited.
1 2 3 4 5 6 7 27 26 25 24 23

walkermathsessentials

LEFT FOOT
LEFT HAND
RIGHT HAND
RIGHT FOOT
Twister

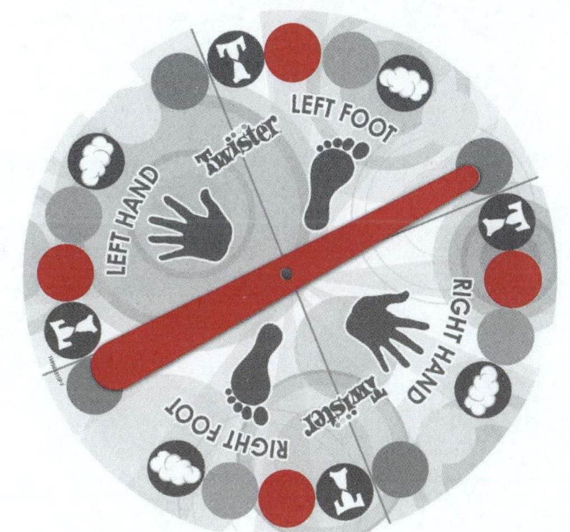

CONTENTS

Glossary

Make your own glossary of key terms:

Term	Definition	Picture/Example
Probability		
Decimal		
Fraction		
Percentage		
Outcome		
Experiment		
Census		
Sample		
Population		
Descriptive variable		

  ISBN: 9780170447256

Term	Definition	Picture/Example
Discrete variable		
Continuous variable		
Frequency		
Axis (plural: axes)		
Mean		
Median		
Mode		
Range		

The statistical inquiry cycle

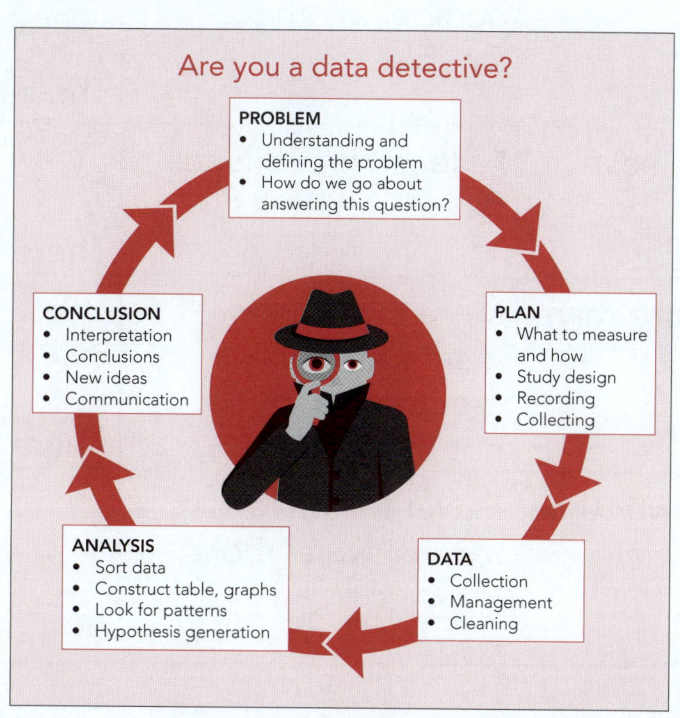

ISBN: 9780170447256

Probability

Useful language

Term	Meaning/use	Example
Equal	The same number of	There is an equal number of glasses and mugs.
Altogether	In total The sum of	Altogether there are four birds.
Half of	One group is half the size of the other.	The number of plants is half the number of scissors.
The difference between	Subtract the number in one group from the number in the other.	There are three cars and one house; the difference is two (3 – 1 = 2).
Twice as many	One number in one group is double the number in other. Double	There are twice as many dogs as cats.
At least	At least three means three or more.	There are at least three flowers.
More than	More than three means anything greater than three, but not three itself.	There are more than three chairs.
Fewer than	Fewer than three means two at most.	or There are fewer than three ice creams.

ISBN: 9780170447256

1 Match the picture to the term. One has been done for you.

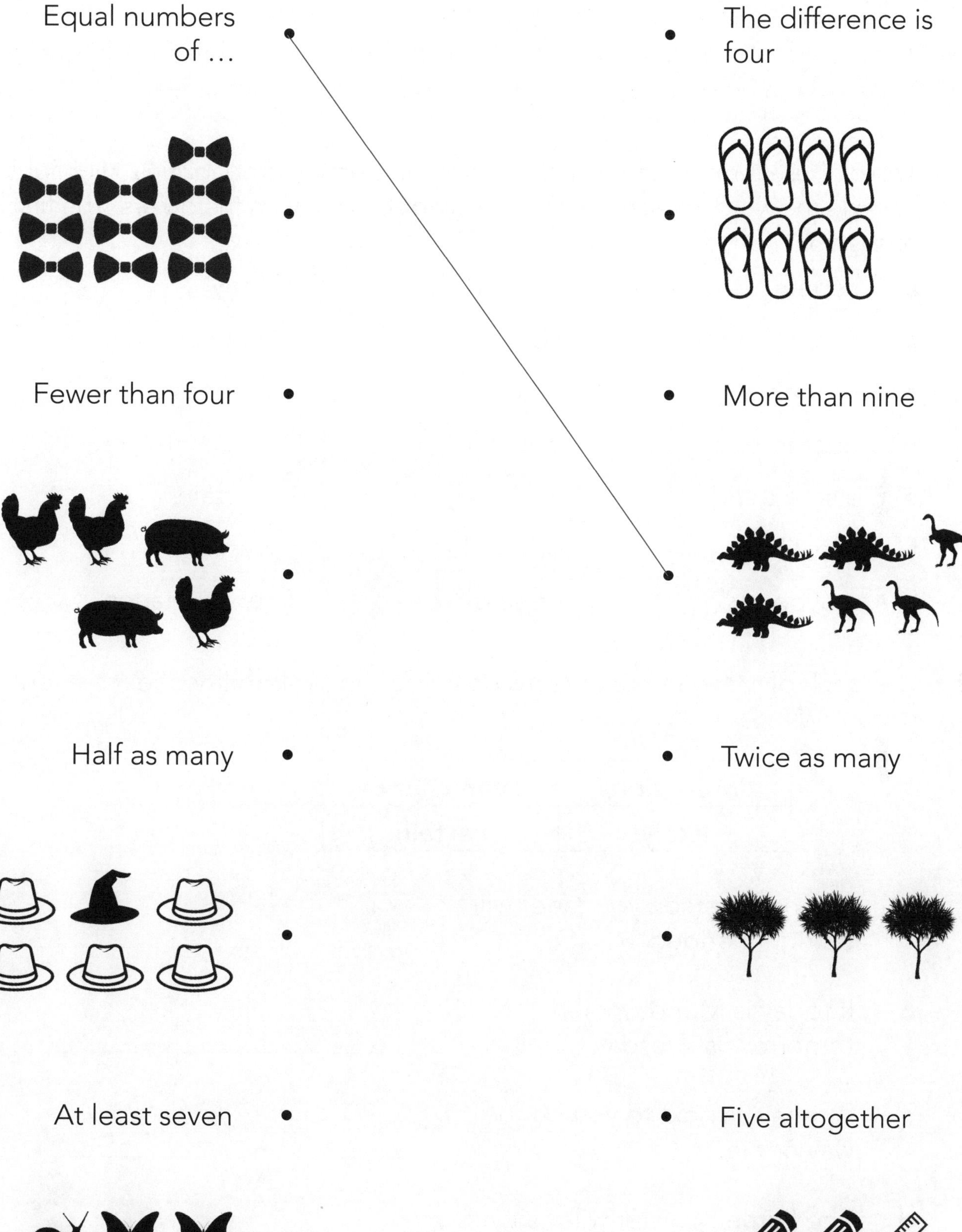

ISBN: 9780170447256

Words used to describe probabilities

- Probability is used to describe **how likely** something is to happen.
- Often we don't know an exact probability, but we make a sensible guess.
- There are many words that are used to describe probabilities.

1 Two of these terms could be used to describe similar probabilities. Highlight or circle the word in each row that does **not** belong with the others. The first one is done for you.

a	certain	definite	maybe
b	almost certain	no way	impossible
c	probable	no chance	impossible
d	guaranteed	possible	slight chance
e	a sure thing	likely	certain
f	very likely	probable	no way
g	maybe	impossible	even chance

2 Use each of these terms once to describe the probability of each event occurring.

impossible	**even chance**	**unlikely**
likely	**certain**	

a The next person you meet will be right handed. ______________________

b If today is Monday, then tomorrow is Tuesday. ______________________

c A moa sits next to you on the way home. ______________________

d The Prime Minister will visit your school tomorrow. ______________________

e Picking a red ball out of a bag that contains two red marbles and two yellow marbles. ______________________

 ISBN: 9780170447256

The probability scale

- A probability value tells us **how likely** it is that an event will occur.
- We use numbers between **0** and **1** to describe probability.

← **Less likely** | **More likely** →

0 — The event will definitely not occur.

0.5 — There is an even chance the event will occur.

1 — The event will definitely occur.

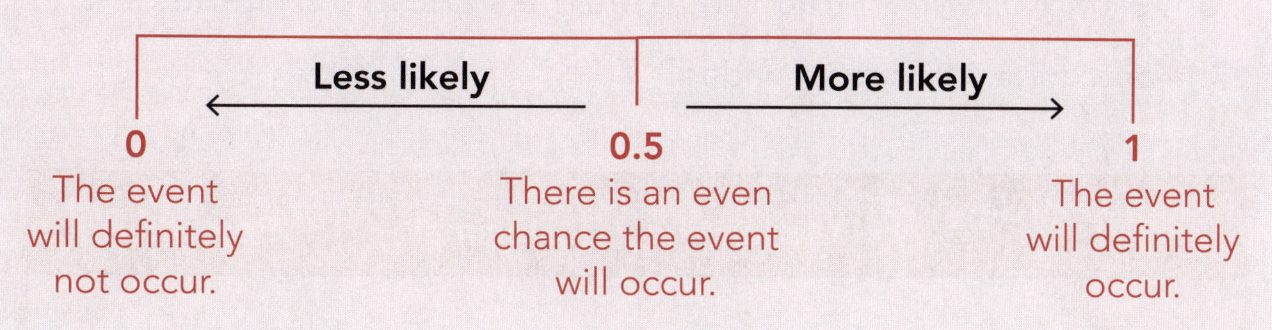

1 Discuss the meanings of these words and terms with your neighbours, and highlight or circle the word that **best** describes the probability value. The first one is done for you.

1	no way	slight chance	**a sure thing**
0.9	impossible	very likely	even chance
0.7	probable	definite	no chance
0.5	certain	even chance	no way
0.3	almost certain	guaranteed	maybe
0.1	slight chance	impossible	good chance
0	no chance	very unlikely	likely

ISBN: 9780170447256

Using numbers to describe probabilities

- Probabilities can be written as **fractions**, **decimals** or **percentages**.

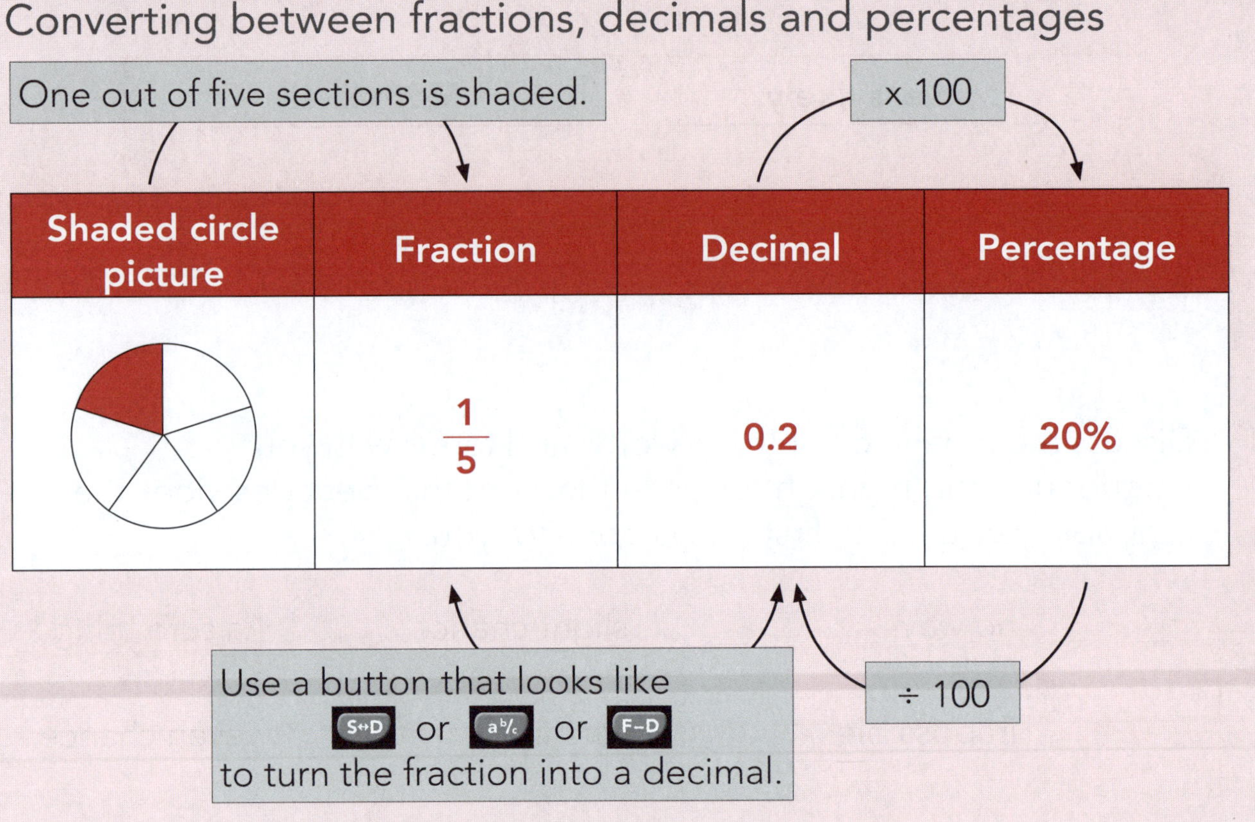

1 Complete this table. Parts have been done for you.

Shaded circle picture	Fraction	Decimal	Percentage
	$\frac{1}{10}$		
		0.2	20%
			25%
	$\frac{3}{10}$		

ISBN: 9780170447256

Shaded circle picture	Fraction	Decimal	Percentage
		$0.33\dot{3}$	$33.\dot{3}\%$
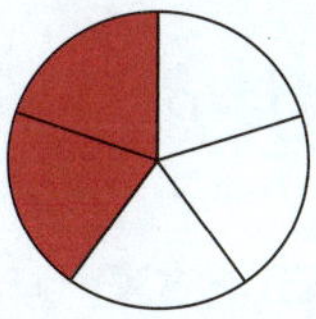			40%
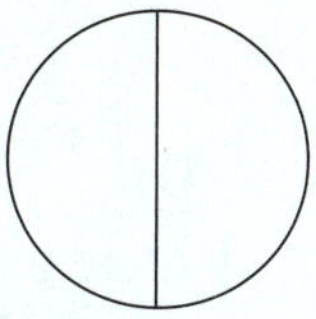	$\frac{5}{10} = \frac{50}{100}$		50%
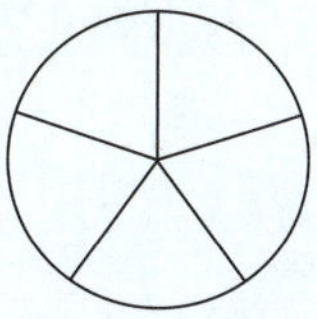		0.6	
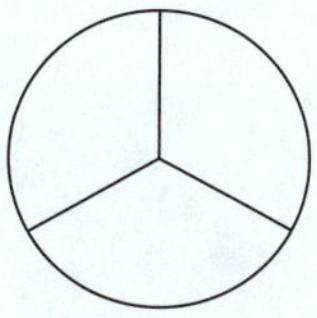		$0.66\dot{6}$	$66.\dot{6}\%$
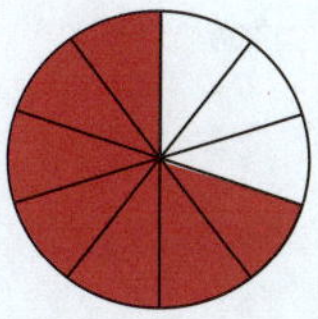	$\frac{7}{10}$		
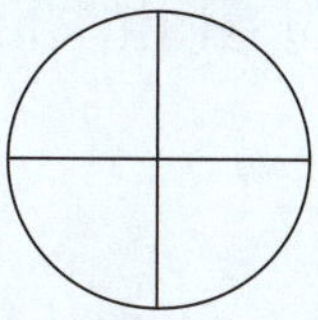	$\frac{3}{4}$		75%
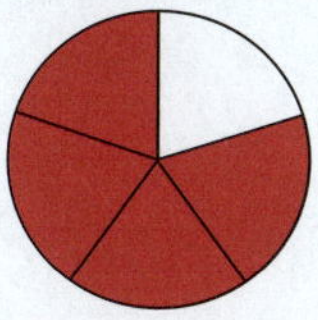		0.8	
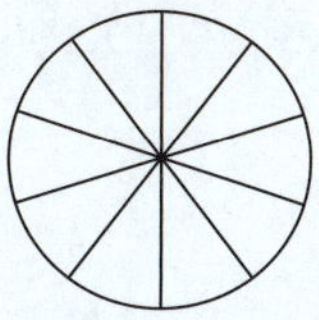			90%

ISBN: 9780170447256

Tools commonly used in probability

- There are several tools that are useful in probability.

Coins

- These are often used in experiments or situations when a probability of 0.5 is needed.
  E.g. which team gets to choose the end they play from in a game.

The probability that a coin lands on its 'head' is 0.5.

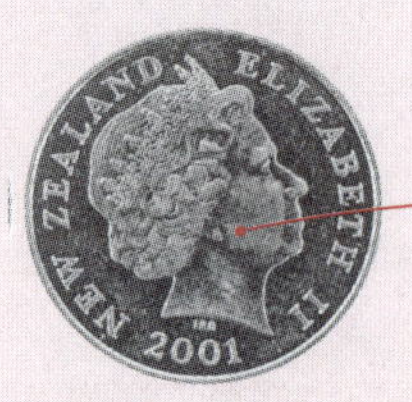

'**Heads**' is the side with the king or queen's head on it.

The probability that a coin lands on its 'tail' is 0.5.

'**Tails**' is the side that does not have the king or queen's head on it.

Dice

- We speak of **several dice**, or **one (single) die**.
- A standard die has six sides.
  There is one number on each side:
  1, 2, 3, 4, 5, 6.

  The probability of rolling each of these numbers is $\frac{1}{6}$.

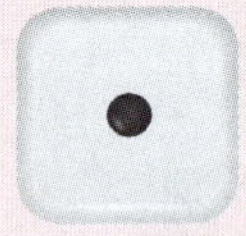  
  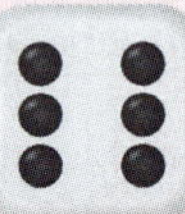

Spinners

- These are sometimes found in board games. The probability of landing on any one of the sectors depends on each spinner.

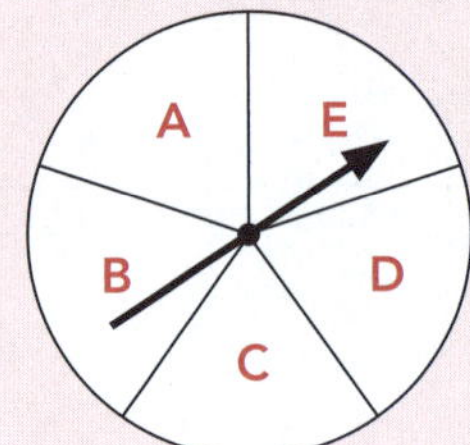

There are 5 equal sectors in this spinner, so the probability of landing on any of these sectors is $\frac{1}{5}$ or 0.2.

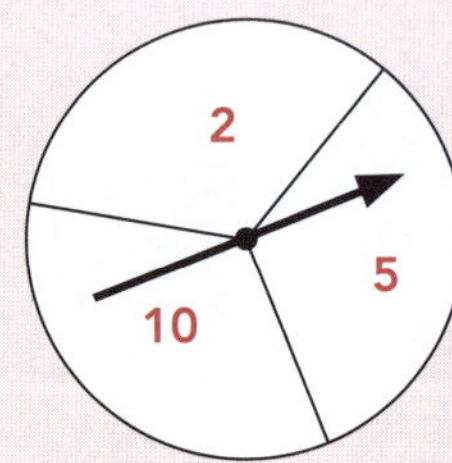

There are 3 equal sectors in this spinner, so the probability of landing on any of these sectors is $\frac{1}{3}$ or $0.\dot{3}$.

ISBN: 9780170447256

Calculating probabilities with one favourable outcome

The number of outcomes we are interested in.

$$\textbf{Probability} = \frac{\textbf{number of 'favourable' outcomes}}{\textbf{number of outcomes in the sample space}}$$

The total number of possible outcomes.

Examples:

1 Hugo has three pencils and two pens in his pencil case. If he picks one out without looking, what is the probability it is a pencil?

$$\text{Probability} = \frac{\text{number of pencils}}{\text{number of items in pencil case}}$$

$P(\text{pencil}) = \frac{3}{5}$ or 0.6

This means the probability of picking a pencil.

2 What is the probability of rolling a 5 on a regular die?

$$\text{Probability} = \frac{\text{number of sides with 5 on them}}{\text{total number of sides on a die}}$$

$P(\text{rolling a 5}) = \frac{1}{6}$ or $0.1\dot{6}$

1 Calculate the probability of this event: tossing a coin and it landing on heads.

$\text{Probability} = \frac{\text{number of heads on a coin}}{\text{number of sides on a coin}} =$ __________

2 When rolling a regular die, calculate the probability of

a rolling a 2: _______________

b rolling a 6: _______________

c rolling a 7: _______________

ISBN: 9780170447256

3 Reggie has six T-shirts in his drawer. He takes one out without looking. What is the probability he pulls out:

a a red T-shirt?

P(red) = $\frac{}{6}$

b a black T-shirt?

P(black) = ____________

c a grey T-shirt?

P(grey) = ____________

4 With this spinner, what is the probability of:

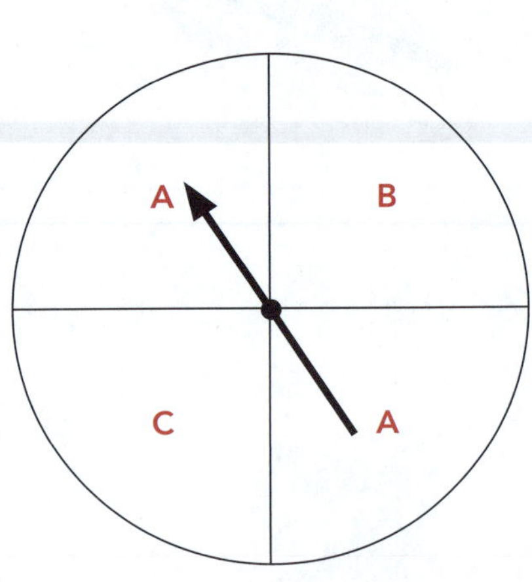

a landing on the letter B? _________

b landing on the letter A? _________

c landing on the letter C? _________

5 Lance has a bag containing two black and three red marbles. If he closed his eyes and picked out a marble, what is the probability that he will get:

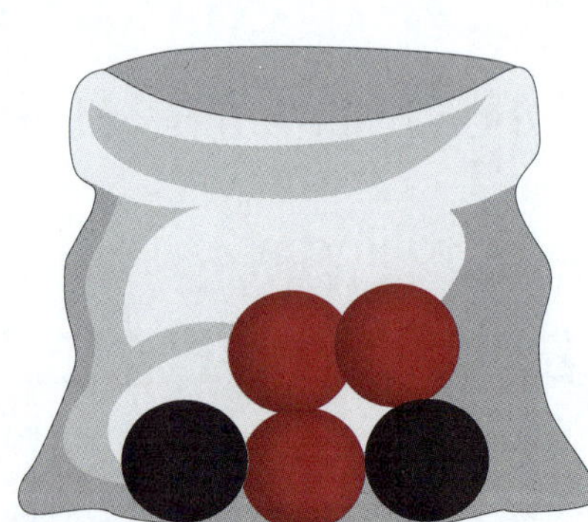

a a black marble? _________

b a red marble? _________

c a yellow marble? _________

 ISBN: 9780170447256

6 Calculate the probability of each event shown at the top of each box if one object is to be selected at random. Then join the dot by the box to the correct probability in the middle. The first one has been done for you.

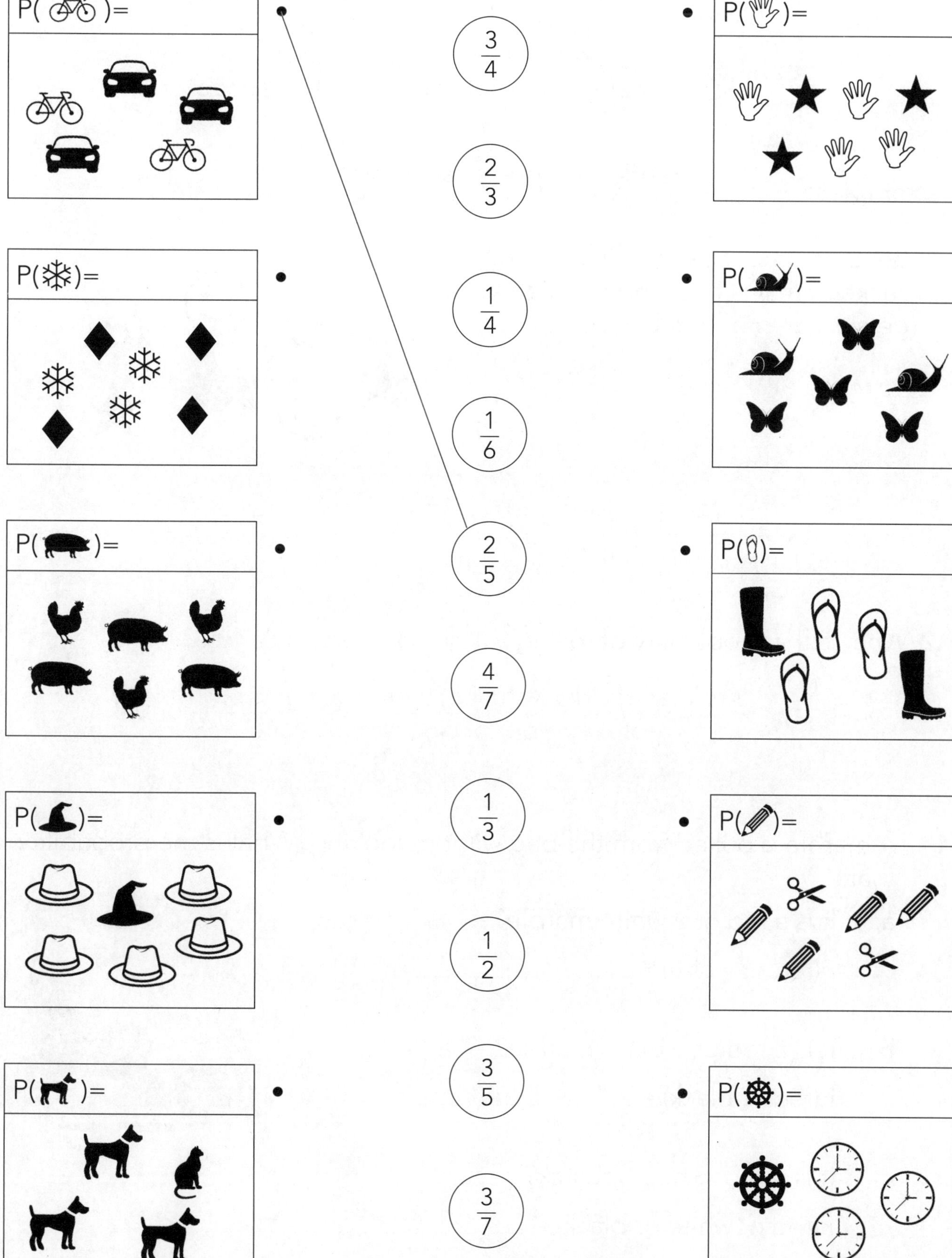

ISBN: 9780170447256

Calculating probabilities with more than one favourable outcome

- When there is more than one favourable outcome, we add them together.

$$\text{Probability} = \frac{\text{outcome 1} + \text{outcome 2}}{\text{total number of objects in the space}}$$

Examples:

Randomly here means without looking or feeling.

1 Beatrice gets to randomly choose a sticker. What is the probability she gets a star or a thumbs up?

$$\text{Probability} = \frac{\text{number of stars} + \text{number of thumbs up}}{\text{total number of stickers}} = \frac{4+1}{7} = \frac{5}{7} \text{ or } 0.7 \text{ (1 dp)}$$

2 What is the probability of rolling a 4 or a 5 on a regular die?

$$\text{Probability} = \frac{\text{number of sides with 4 or 5 on them}}{\text{total number of sides}} = \frac{2}{6} = \frac{1}{3} \text{ or } 0.\dot{3}$$

1 A marble is pulled from the bag without looking. What is the probability that:

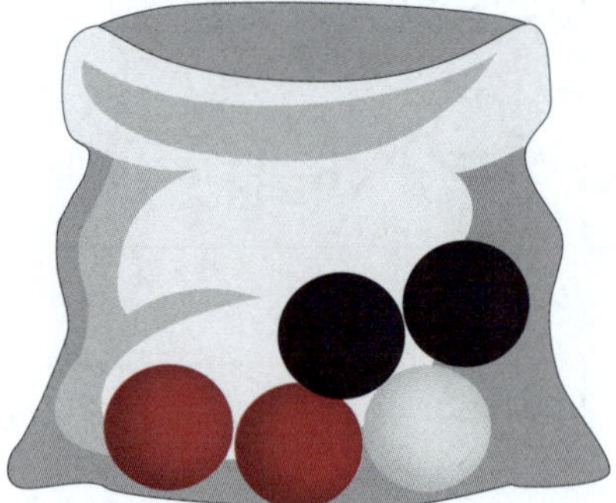

a it is a red or a white marble?

P(red or white) = ________________

b it is a red or a black marble?

P(red or black) = ________________

c it is red or white or black?

P(red or white or black) = ________________

 ISBN: 9780170447256

2 Lucy's father has six ties in his closet. He asks her to pick one at random. What is the probability that:

a she picks a tie with stripes?

P(stripes) = $\frac{1 + 1}{\quad}$ =

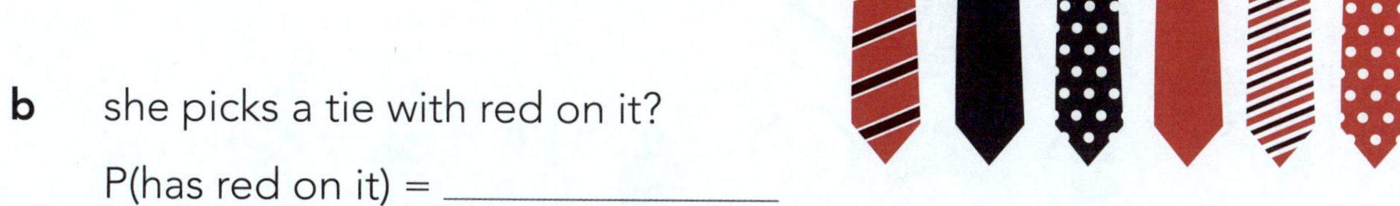

b she picks a tie with red on it?

P(has red on it) = ______________

c she picks a tie with stripes or dots?

P(stripes or dots) = ______________

d she picks a tie that has red or black?

P(red or black) = ______________

3 With this spinner, what are these probabilities?

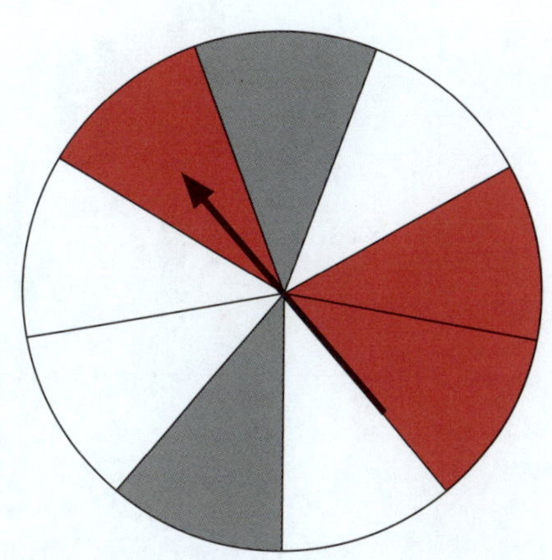

a P(red or grey) = ______________

b P(white or grey) = ______________

c P(red or grey or white) = ______________

4 When rolling a regular die, calculate the probability of rolling

a a 2 or a 3: ______________

b an odd number: ______________

c an even number: ______________

d not a 6: ______________

e a number more than 4: ______________

Calculate the probability of each event shown in each box at right if **one** object is to be selected at random from each group. The first one has been done for you.

5

a P(or) = $\frac{3}{10}$

b P(or) =

c P(or) =

6

B A N X A
A U U A
N X A

a P(N or X) =

b P(A or N or B) =

c P(vowel) =

7

a P(or) =

b P(or) =

c P(or or) =

8

6 7 2 1 3 2 1
2 3 6 1 6 2

a P(2 or 1) =

b P(even number) =

c P(number more than 5) =

ISBN: 9780170447256

Calculating probabilities for more than one event

- When there is more than one event, **probability trees** and **tables** are useful ways of creating **lists** to help you calculate probabilities.

Example:

List

Two coins are tossed at the same time. What are the possible outcomes?

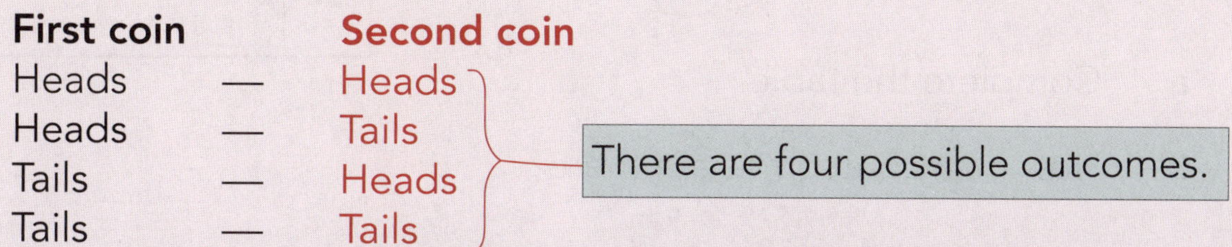

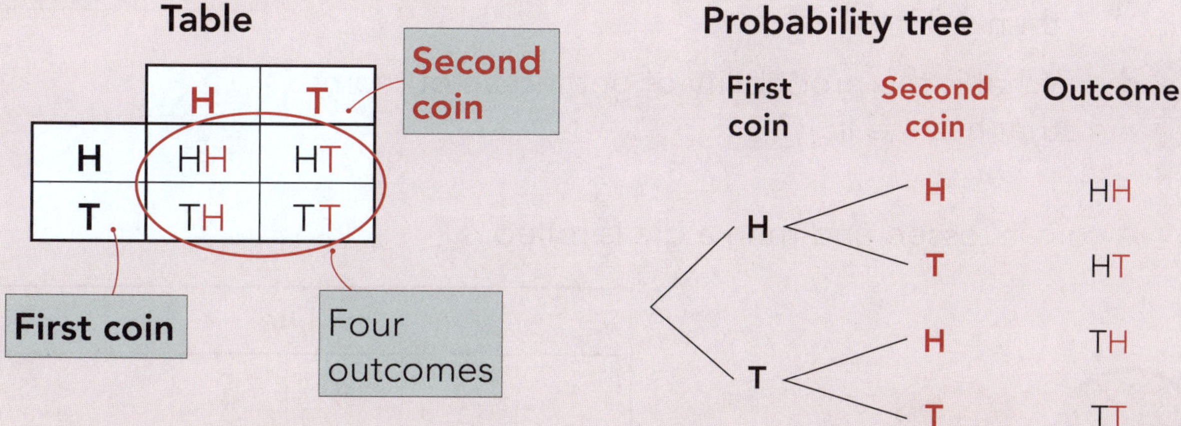

The probability of any one of these outcomes happening is $\frac{1}{4}$.

What is the probability of getting Heads, Heads? $P = \frac{1}{4} = 0.25$

What is the probability of getting one of each? $P = \frac{2}{4} = \frac{1}{2} = 0.5$

Notice that there are two ways of getting one of each: HT or TH.

What is the probability of getting Tails, Tails, Tails? $P = 0$

There are only two events, so this is impossible.

ISBN: 9780170447256

Answer the following questions.

1 A coin is tossed and then the spinner is spun.

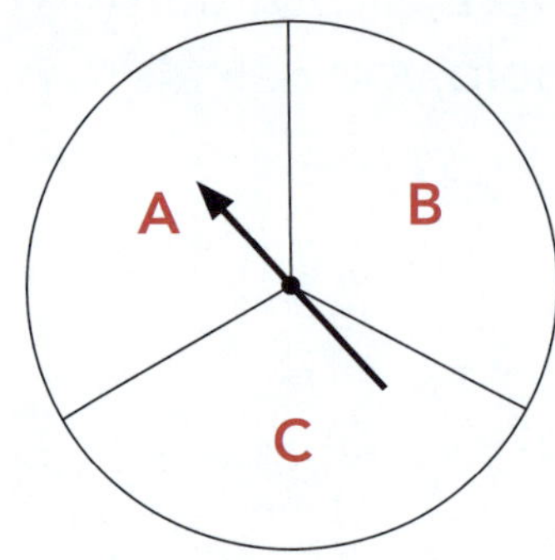

		Spinner		
		A	B	
Coin	H			
				TC

a Complete the table.

b How many outcomes are there? __________

c What is the probability of getting Tails and then a B? __________

d What is the probability of getting an outcome that has a C in it? __________

2 A coin is tossed and then a die is rolled.

		Die					
		1	2	3	4	5	6
Coin	H				H4		
	T		T2				

a Complete the table.

b How many outcomes are there? __________

c What is the probability of getting the outcome H5? __________

d How many outcomes have a 6 in them? __________

e What is the probability of getting an outcome with a T in it? __________

ISBN: 9780170447256

3 A coin is tossed and this spinner is spun.

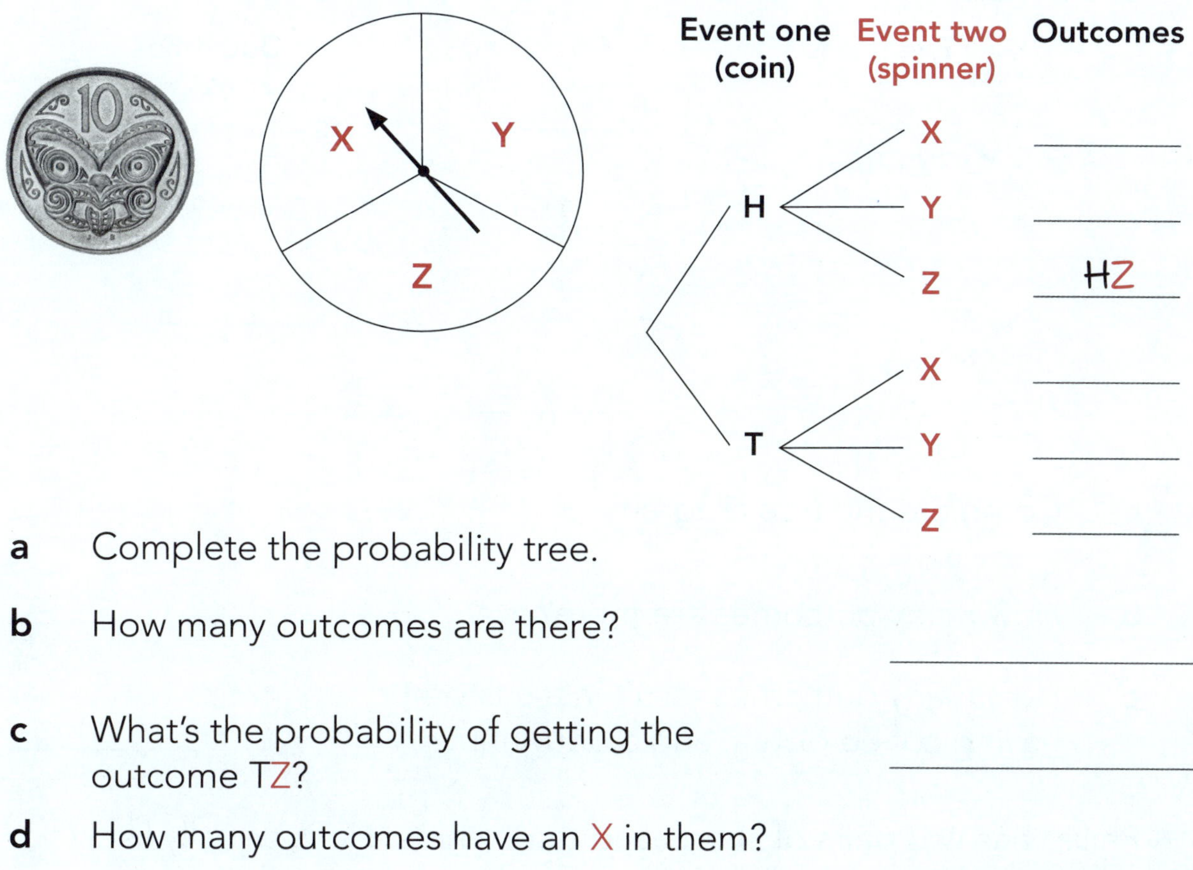

a Complete the probability tree.

b How many outcomes are there? ______

c What's the probability of getting the outcome TZ? ______

d How many outcomes have an X in them? ______

4 As guests arrive at a Christmas party, they are given a red or green hat and a silver or gold cracker. They are equally likely to get red or green hats and equally likely to get silver or gold crackers.

		Crackers	
		Silver	**Gold**
Hats	**Red**	RS	
	Green		

a Complete the table.

b How many outcomes are there? ______

c What is the probability that a guest gets a red hat and a gold cracker? ______

d What is the probability that a guest gets a silver cracker? ______

ISBN: 9780170447256

5 At a café, customers can choose either coffee or tea, and then a scone or a donut.

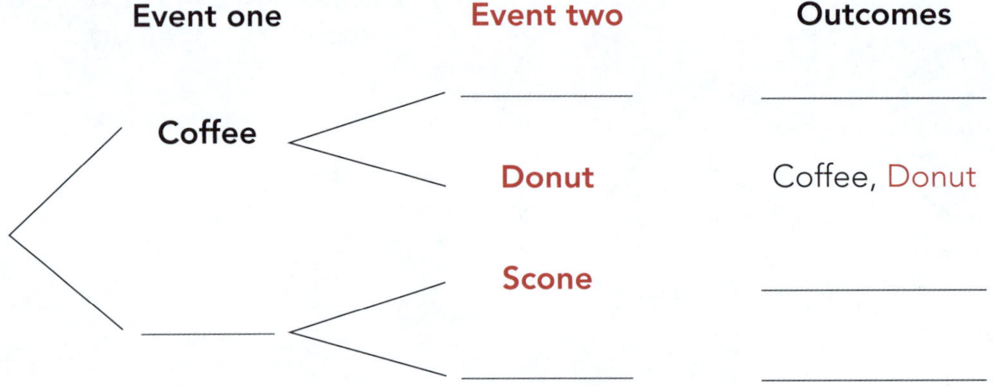

a Complete the tree diagram.

b How many outcomes are there? ______

c How many outcomes result in a customer having coffee or tea, and a doughnut? ______

6 Phillip has two pairs of shorts and three shirts. He is equally likely to wear any shirt or any of the pairs of shorts.

		Shirt		
		Yellow	Red	White
Shorts	Black			
	Grey			

a Complete the table.

b What colour shorts does he own? ______

c How many different outfits can Phillip wear? ______

d What is the probability that he wears a yellow shirt? ______

e What is the probability that he wears a yellow or red shirt with grey shorts? ______

 ISBN: 9780170447256

Probability experiments

- Where we do not know the probabilities of events, we can do either a **survey** or an **experiment**.
- Experiments are used to **estimate** probabilities. The outcomes are likely to differ each time the experiment is repeated.

Example:

Harry tosses a coin 10 times.
Here is his outcome: **H, H, T, H, H, H, H, T, H, T** — He got 7 heads.

Hailey also tossed a coin 10 times.
Here is her outcome: **T, H, T, T, T, H, H, T, T, H** — She got 4 heads.

The outcomes of these two experiments are different from one another.

If we repeated this experiment lots of times, we would expect that **on average** we would get 5 heads.

Answer the following questions.

1 Harry's teacher decided that it would be good to test this with the whole class. She organised for all 25 students to each toss a coin 10 times. Their combined results are shown in this table.

	Number	Probability	
Heads	120	$\frac{120}{250}$	
Tails			0.52
Totals	250	1	1

a Complete the table.

b Do you think that these results prove that when a coin is tossed, the probability of getting a head is not 0.5? Yes/No
Explain why or why not.

____

____

ISBN: 9780170447256

c Here are the results of Ari's first nine tosses: **T, H, H, T, H, H, H, H, H**.

Harry said that because his last five tosses were heads, the next toss would almost certainly be a tail. Do you agree with Harry? Yes/No
Explain why or why not.

____

d How many heads would you expect to get if you tossed a coin 1000 times? ____________

2 Gilbert rolled a regular die six times.

a How many times would you expect him to roll a 3? ____________

b Here are his results: **3, 1, 3, 4, 2, 6**.
How many times did he roll a 3? ____________

c Was that more or fewer than you expected? ____________

d Bert rolled a die 10 times. Here are the results:
4, 1, 5, 4, 6, 3, 2, 4, 4, 4.

Harry said that because Bert had rolled five 4s in 10 rolls, the next roll would almost certainly not be a 4. Do you agree with Harry? Yes/No

Explain why or why not.

____

e How many fours would you expect to get if you rolled a die 600 times? ____________

3 A spinner was spun six times.

Red
Blue
Green

a How many times would you expect it to land on green? ____________

b Here are the results:

Red, Blue, Red, Red, Green, Red.

How many times did it land on green? ____________

c Was that more or fewer than you expected? ____________

d How many times would you expect it to land on green if you spun it 300 times? ____________

  ISBN: 9780170447256

Comparing decimals

- If you want to **compare** probabilities, it is usually easiest to convert them to **decimals**, and then compare them.

Deciding which is the larger of a pair of decimals

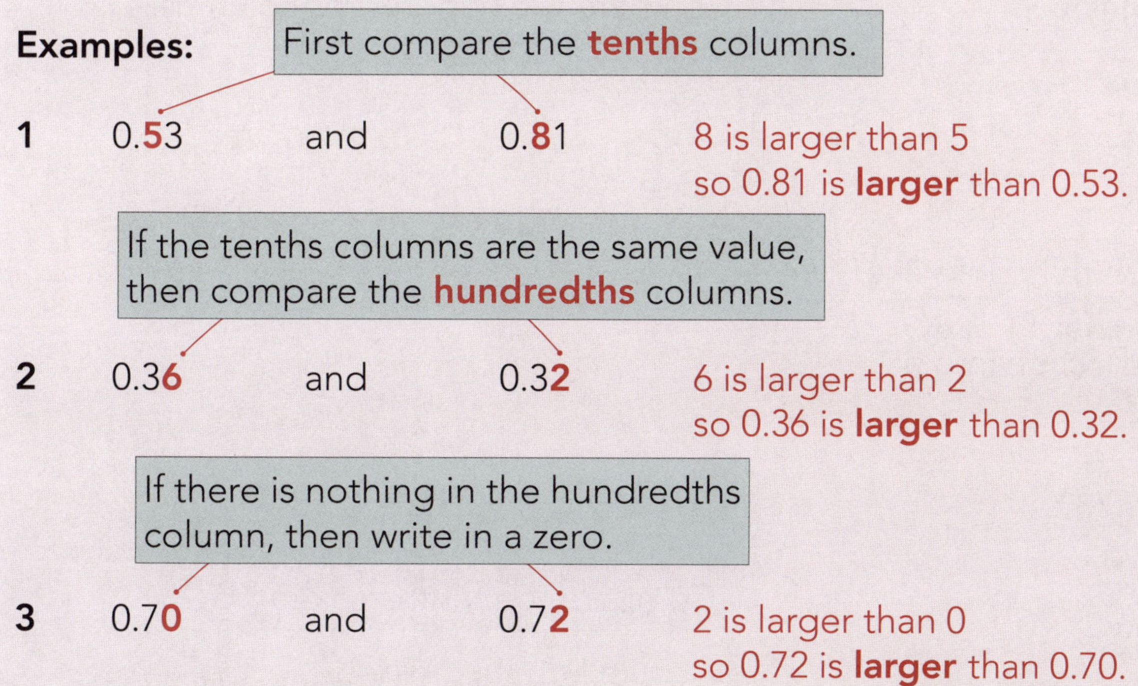

1 Highlight the value that is the larger of each pair.

a	0.93	0.52	**b**	0.49	0.73
c	0.54	0.58	**d**	0.91	0.90
e	0.67	0.76	**f**	0.4	0.47

2 From the table below, select the most appropriate point for each position on the number line.

0.85	0.41	0.25	0.76
0.11	0.3	0.54	0.6

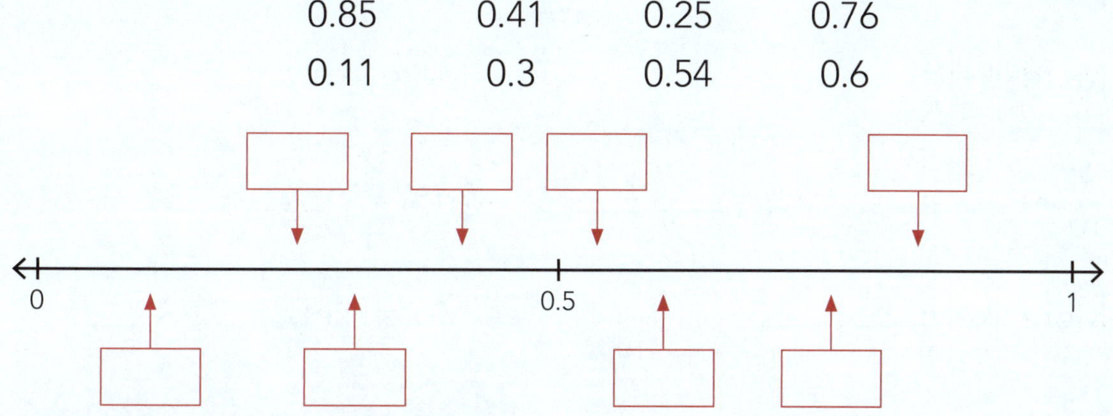

ISBN: 9780170447256

Comparing probabilities

- Convert probabilities to **decimals**, and then compare them.

Deciding which is the more likely of a pair of probabilities

Examples:

Compare the hundredths columns.

1 $\frac{1}{4}$ or $\frac{1}{5}$ $\qquad \frac{1}{4} = 0.25 \qquad \frac{1}{5} = 0.2 = 0.20$

Use a button that looks like S↔D or a b/c or F–D to turn the fraction into a decimal.

5 is larger than 0, so $\frac{1}{4}$ is more likely than $\frac{1}{5}$.

2 $\frac{2}{3}$ or 73% $\qquad \frac{2}{3} = 0.66\dot{6} \qquad 73\% = 0.73$

÷100

Compare the tenths columns.

7 is larger than 6, so 73% is more likely than $\frac{2}{3}$.

Convert these probabilities into decimals and state which is more likely.

1 $\frac{1}{4}$ = ________ 0.3 = ________

More likely: ________

2 85% = ________ 0.82 = ________

More likely: ________

3 25% = ________ $\frac{1}{3}$ = ________

More likely: ________

4 0.5 = ________ $\frac{2}{5}$ = ________

More likely: ________

5 $\frac{9}{10}$ = ________ 92% = ________

More likely: ________

6 61% = ________ 0.6 = ________

More likely: ________

 ISBN: 9780170447256

7 $\frac{4}{5}$ = ________ $\frac{2}{3}$ = ________

More likely: ________

8 $\frac{1}{3}$ = ________ 30% = ________

More likely: ________

9 $\frac{1}{9}$ = ________ 10% = ________

More likely: ________

10 $\frac{11}{20}$ = ________ 0.5 = ________

More likely: ________

Convert these probabilities into decimals and place them in ascending order (least likely to most likely).

11 $\frac{3}{5}$ = ________

0.59 = ________

61% = ________

________ ________ ________

Least likely Most likely

12 18% = ________

$\frac{1}{6}$ = ________

0.2 = ________

________ ________ ________

Least likely Most likely

13 33% = ________

$\frac{1}{3}$ = ________

0.34 = ________

________ ________ ________

Least likely Most likely

ISBN: 9780170447256

Challenge 1

1 To win a prize, the spinner has to land on **A**. You are given the choice of two spinners. Which one would you choose? __________________

Spinner 1 **Spinner 2**

Explain your answer. ______________________________

____

____

2 Without looking, you pull a ball out of one of these bags. If you pull out a red ball, you win a prize. You are given the choice of two bags.

Which bag would you choose? __________

Bag A **Bag B**

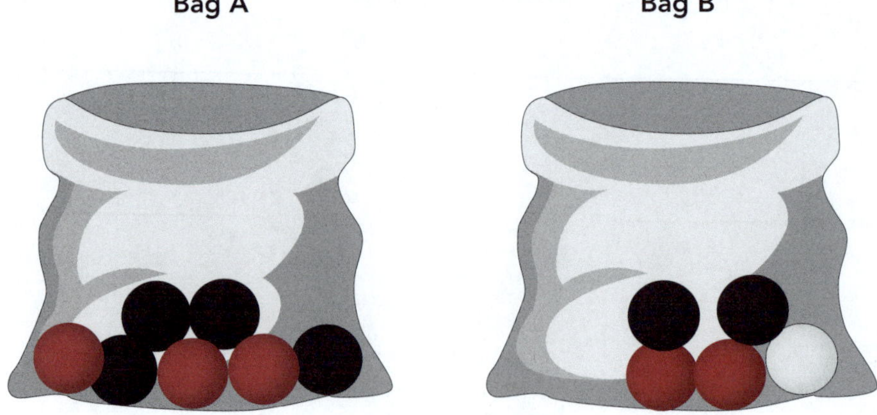

Explain your answer. ______________________________

____

____

  ISBN: 9780170447256

Statistical concepts

- It's important to understand some terms and concepts that are important in Statistics.

Census and sample

A census compared with a sample

Census
- You collect data from **every member of the population**.
- You get very accurate information.
- However, it is often impossible and usually very expensive to do.
- It is best to do a census if the answer to the question **really matters**.
- In New Zealand, a census of the population takes place every five years.

Sample
- You collect data from **just some of the population**.
- The information you get will not be as accurate.
- However, it is much easier and cheaper to take a sample.
- It's important that the sample is selected ***fairly***.

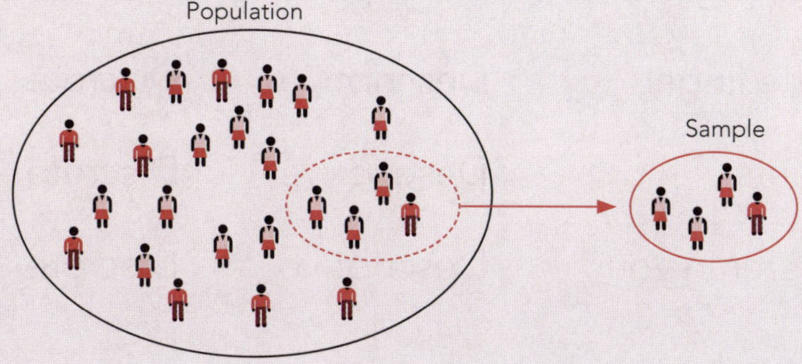

Which would be more appropriate to answer these questions and why?

	Question	Census or sample?	Why?
1	What is the New Zealand's favourite TV programme?		
2	Should New Zealand change its captial city?		

ISBN: 9780170447256

Types of variables

There are three type of variables:

Descriptive variables	These are **descriptions** or **names**. Data recorded about each person/thing: **words**. Typical question starts with 'What …' **Examples:** colour, type of pet, favourite something.
Discrete variables	These are **numbers** which are the result of **counting**. Data recorded about each person/thing: **whole numbers**. Typical question starts with 'How many …' **Examples:** number of pets, number of T-shirts.
Continuous variables	These **numbers** are the result of **measuring**. They can be **fractions** or **decimals**. Typical question starts with 'How long, heavy, etc. …' **Examples:** height, weight, distance, time.

Identify which type of variable these are and highlight the correct term.

1	Favourite clothing brand	Descriptive	Discrete	Continuous
2	Length of little finger	Descriptive	Discrete	Continuous
3	Number of pets	Descriptive	Discrete	Continuous
4	Volume of water in your drink bottle	Descriptive	Discrete	Continuous

Here is some data that has been collected:

Question		**Sam**	**Noah**	**Kauri**	**Neve**
A	How many siblings do you have?	2	0	4	1
B	How long is your hand?	160 mm	158 mm	147 mm	152 mm
C	What is your favourite colour?	Blue	Orange	Green	Yellow

5	Question A's answers are	Descriptive	Discrete	Continuous
6	Question B's answers are	Descriptive	Discrete	Continuous
7	Question C's answers are	Descriptive	Discrete	Continuous

ISBN: 9780170447256

Data display

- There are different ways of displaying data. Which is most appropriate depends on the **type** of variable.

1 Match these types of graphs to the images below. One has been done for you.

French	||||
German	~~||||~~ ||||
Latin	||
Spanish	~~||||~~

Frequency table

Strip graph

Pictogram

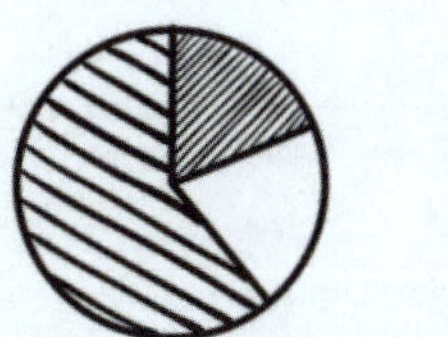

Bar graph

Soccer	Badminton	Netball	Hockey	Rugby league	Rugby union

Line graph

Pie chart

Pet	Frequency
(dog)	5
(fish)	3
(cat)	7

Tally chart

Dot plot

ISBN: 9780170447256

Tally charts and frequency tables

- Tally charts are used when you are counting **descriptive** or **discrete** variables.
- You add the tallies to get the frequencies.

Understanding tally charts and frequency tables

As you count, each new object is recorded by adding a 'stick'.

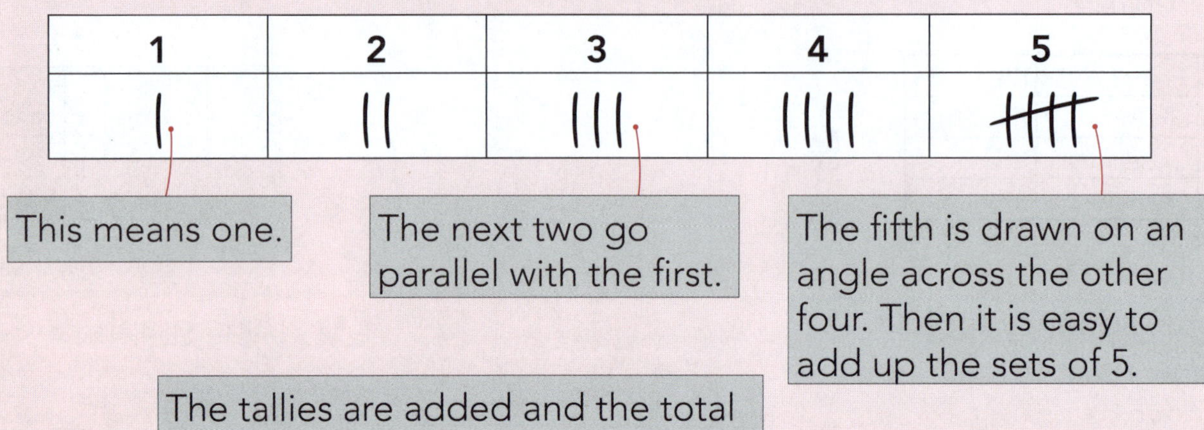

Example: The tallies are added and the total is written in the frequency column.

Favourite thing to do on a rainy day	**Tally**	**Frequency**
Read a book	𝍸	5
Do a puzzle	𝍷𝍷𝍷	3
Play video games	𝍸 𝍷𝍷	7
Watch a movie	𝍸 𝍸	10

How many people prefer to watch a movie? 10

How many people like to read or do a puzzle? 5 + 3 = 8

What was the least favourite activity? Doing a puzzle

ISBN: 9780170447256

Answer the following questions.

1 Students were asked which item they would choose on a hot day.

Item	Tally	Frequency
Ice cream	𝍸 𝍸 |	
Milkshake	𝍸 ||	7
Ice block	|||	
Drink	||||	

a Complete the table.

b What was the most popular item? __________

c What was the least popular item? __________

d How many students wanted either an ice cream or an ice block? __________

e How many students did not want an ice cream? __________

f Calculate the probability that a student preferred a drink. __________

g The probability that a student preferred a milkshake = 0.28. What is the probability that a student did not want a milkshake? __________

h What percentage of students wanted ice creams? __________

ISBN: 9780170447256

2 Students were asked which ball they would like to play with.

Item	Tally	Frequency
Soccer ball	𝍸	
Rugby ball	𝍸 𝍸 |||	
Basketball	𝍸 ||||	

a Complete the table.

b How many students wanted a soccer ball or a basketball? __________

c What was the most popular ball? __________

d How many students were asked? __________

3 Jeremiah listed the items he sold during an hour in his parents' bakery.

Item	Tally	Frequency
Pies	𝍸 𝍸 |	
Filled rolls	𝍸 𝍸 𝍸 𝍸 |	
Cream buns	𝍸 𝍸 𝍸 |||	

a Complete the table.

b What was the most popular item? __________

c How many items did he sell? __________

d What percentage of the items he sold were filled rolls? __________

 ISBN: 9780170447256

Creating tally charts and frequency tables

Example: Students were asked what their favourite fruit was.

Here are the results:

Item	Tally	Frequency
	卌	5
	|	1
	||	2
	||||	4
	Total	**12**

Cross out each object when you add its tally stroke.

Adding the total is sensible.

4 **a** What was the least popular fruit? ____________

b How many students preferred fruit with edible skin? ____________

c What is the probability that a student preferred oranges? ____________

ISBN: 9780170447256

5 Karina and her classmates wrote down what their first pet was.

a Complete the tally chart. The first two have been done for you.

Item	Tally	Frequency
	|	
	|	

	Total	

b What was the most popular first pet? __________

c How many classmates does she have? __________

d What percentage of her classmates had a rabbit as their first pet? __________

  ISBN: 9780170447256

Pictographs

- Pictographs use pictures to show **descriptive** and **discrete** data.
- Assume each picture represents one person or thing unless you are told otherwise.

Understanding pictographs

Example: Sarah listed what animals she found in a large rock pool.

Item	
Starfish	★ ★ ★
Crab	🦀 🦀 🦀 🦀 🦀
Fish	🐟 🐟
Sea snail	🐚 🐚 🐚 🐚

What was the most common creature in the rock pool? Crab

How many starfish were there? 3

How many creatures did Sarah find altogether? 14

1 Jacob noted what footwear people were wearing as they walked by.

Footwear	
Gumboots	👢 👢
Jandals	🩴 🩴 🩴
Sneakers	👟 👟 👟 👟 👟 👟
High heels	👠
No shoes	👣 👣 👣

a How many people were wearing sneakers? ______________

b What was the least common of the footwear seen by Jacob? ______________

c How many people were wearing some kind of footwear? ______________

ISBN: 9780170447256

2 While gardening, Harriet noted what insects she saw.

Insects	
Fly	
Beetle	
Butterfly	
Dragonfly	
Bee	

a What was the most common insect? ____________

b How many butterflies did Harriet see? ____________

c How many beetles and bees did she see? ____________

3 Casey watched the types of vehicle going past her house.

Vehicle	
Car	
Bike	
Bus	
Motorbike	
Truck	

a How many buses went past? ____________

b What was the most common type of vehicle? ____________

c Casey is twice as likely to see a truck as a ________________.

 ISBN: 9780170447256

Completing pictographs

- When creating pictographs, use pictures that are simple to draw and easy to copy.
- Every picture should be about the same size.
- Pictures should be a similar size and lined up in columns.

Example: A group of teachers wrote down whether they used contact lenses, glasses or neither for reading.

~~Glasses~~	~~Neither~~	~~Glasses~~	~~Glasses~~
~~Contact lenses~~	~~Glasses~~	~~Contact lenses~~	~~Glasses~~
~~Glasses~~	~~Neither~~	~~Glasses~~	~~Contact lenses~~

Item	
Contact lenses	☺ ☺ ☺
Glasses	☺ ☺ ☺ ☺ ☺ ☺ ☺
Neither	☺ ☺

Cross out each word when you add its symbol.

4 Students were asked what their favourite subject at school was. Complete the pictograph.

~~Science~~	~~Science~~	Mathematics	Art
English	Art	English	Art
Science	Art	Mathematics	Music

Subject	
English	
Science	♥ ♥
Mathematics	
Music	
Art	

Pie graphs

- Pie graphs are appropriate for **descriptive** data.
- They are best used when there are relatively few divisions of the data.
- The area of each sector is proportional to the frequency of each variable. This means that the biggest group has the biggest sector.

Understanding pie graphs

Examples:

1 Here are some common reasons students use for not doing their homework.

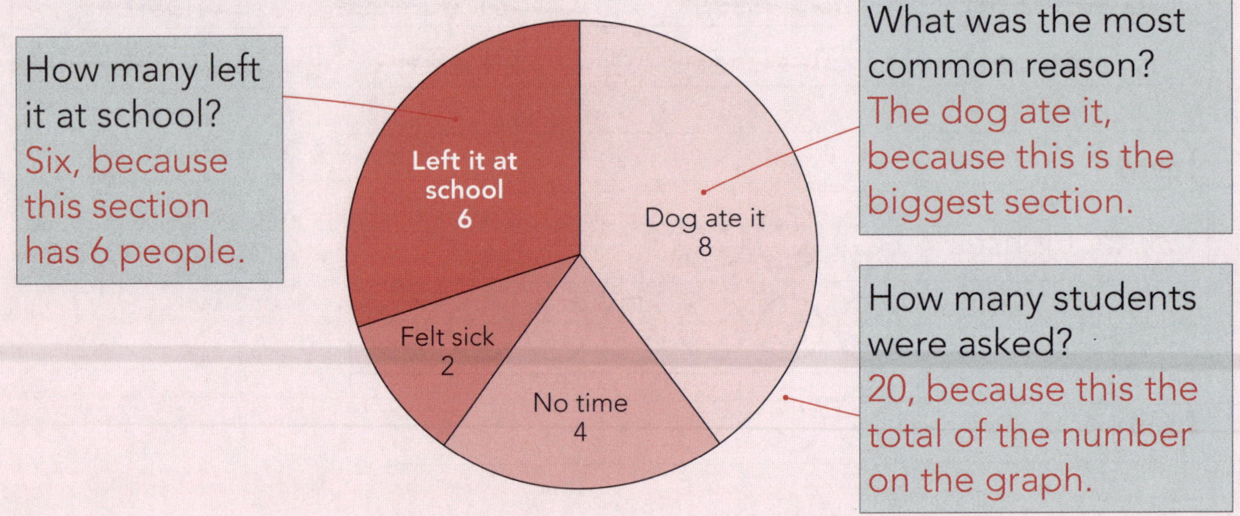

Sometimes you will know how many were surveyed and will have to calculate answers to questions.

2 Sixteen students were asked what they mostly did after school yesterday.

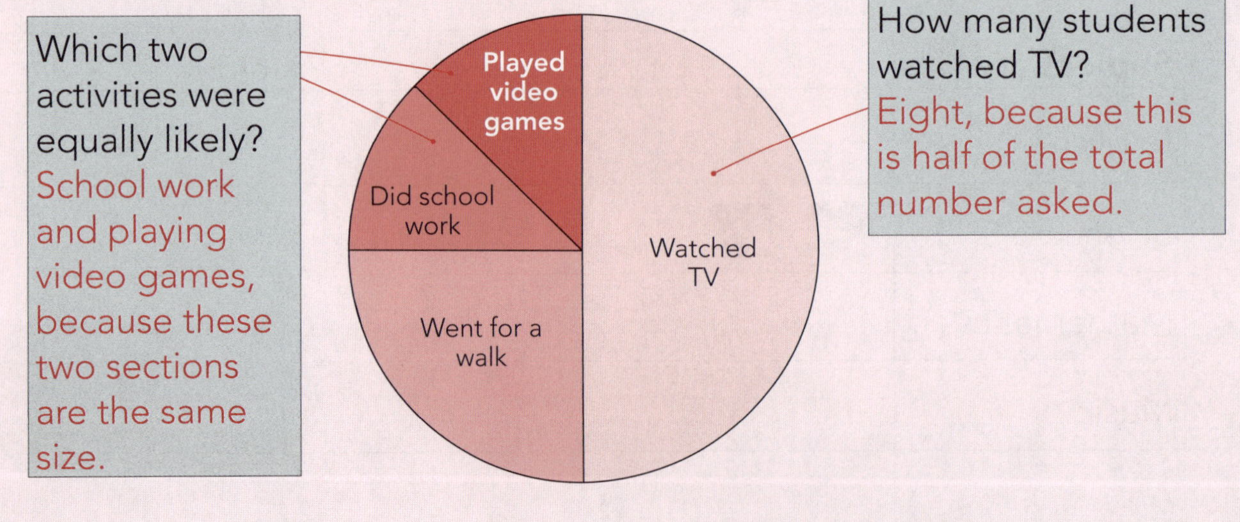

ISBN: 9780170447256

1 Grace asked her friends what their favourite fruit was.

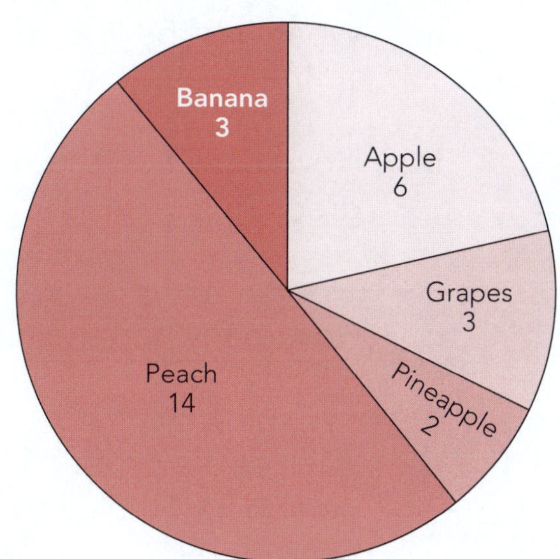

a How many preferred apples or grapes?

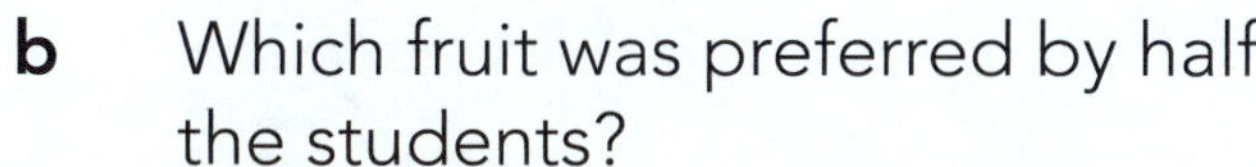

b Which fruit was preferred by half the students?

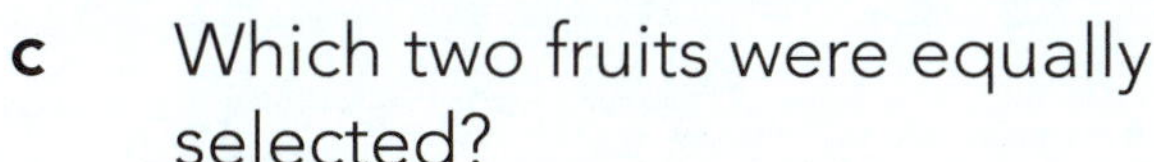

c Which two fruits were equally selected?

d How many friends did Grace ask?

e What fraction of the students preferred apples?

2 George went for a walk in the bush and noted the birds he saw.

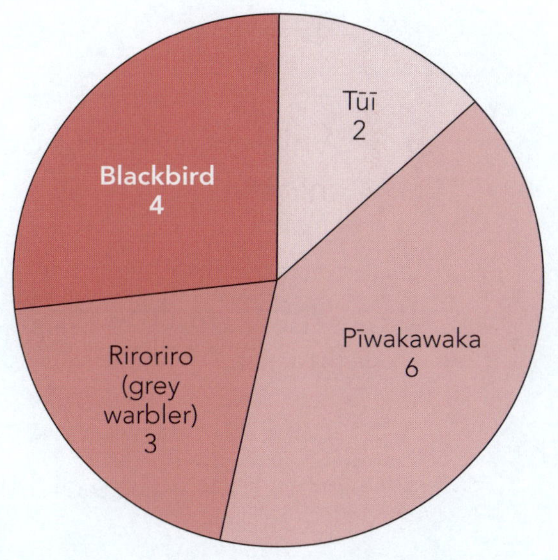

a Which bird did he see the most?

b Which bird did he see the least?

c Which bird did he see half as often as pīwakawaka?

d How many birds did he see that were not blackbirds?

e What percentage of the birds that he saw were pīwakawaka?

f What fraction of the birds were either riroriro or tūī?

ISBN: 9780170447256

3 Twenty people got their nails done at the local salon.

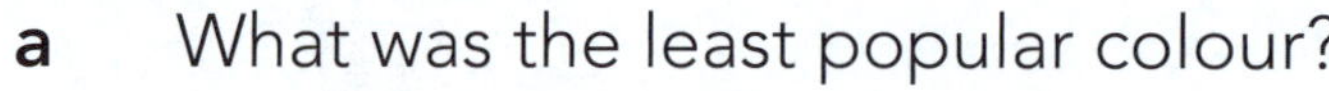

a What was the least popular colour?

____

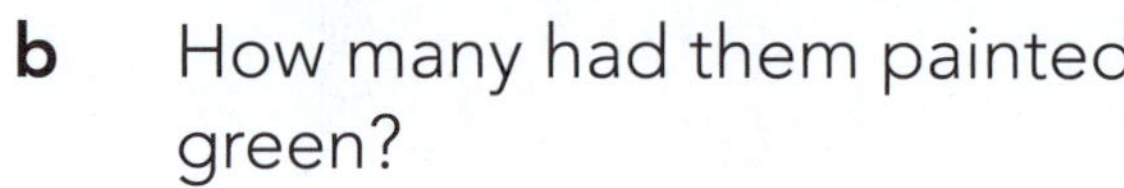

b How many had them painted green?

____

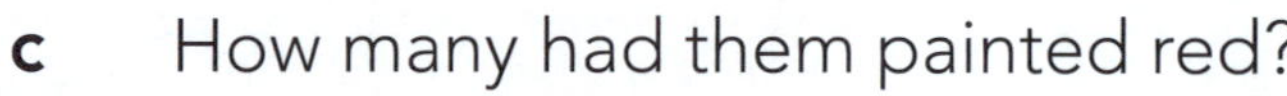

c How many had them painted red?

____

d What is the probability that a person had their nails painted black or red?

____

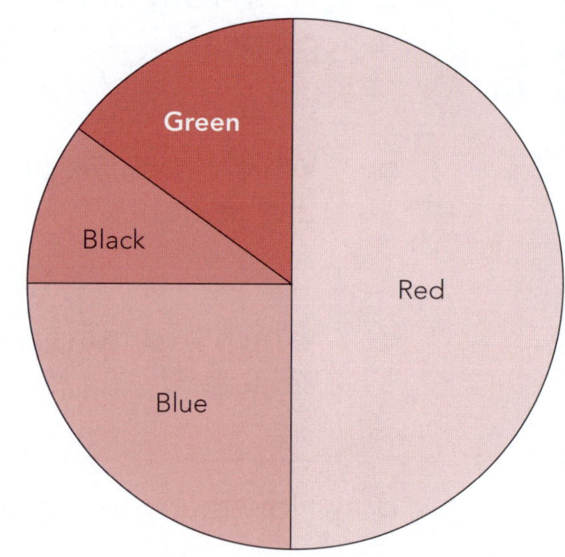

4 The school canteen recorded which pies were being sold.

a Which pie flavour was bought the most?

____

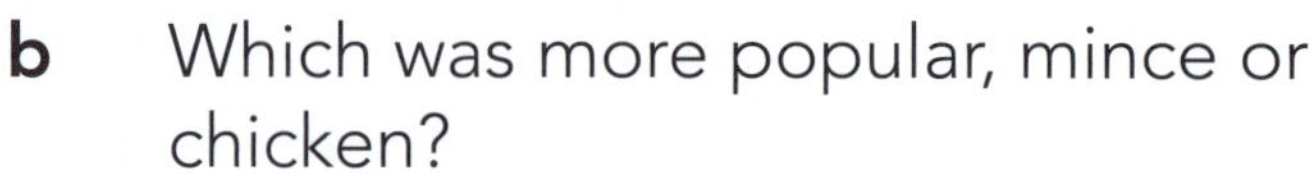

b Which was more popular, mince or chicken?

____

c Which was the least popular flavour?

____

d How many pies did they sell?

____

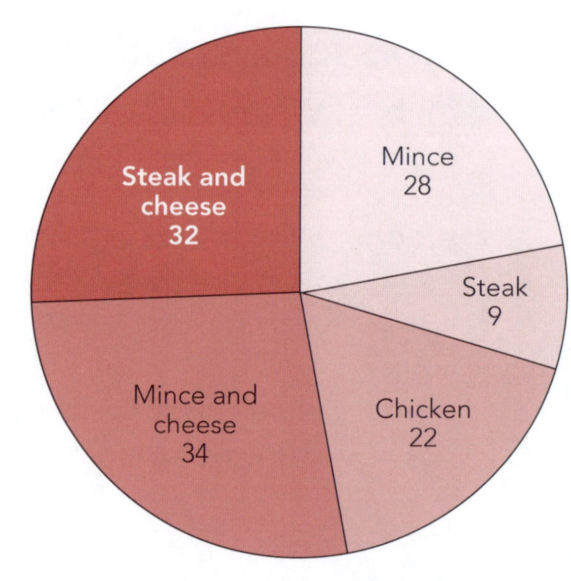

e Based on this data, what is the probability that the next pie they sell will be a mince pie? ______________________

f Based on this data, what is the probability that the next pie they sell will be a mince or chicken pie? ______________________

 ISBN: 9780170447256

Completing pie graphs

5 Eight students were asked which sport each would rather play at lunchtime. Five said they wanted to play cricket and the rest were keen to play touch.
Complete the pie graph.

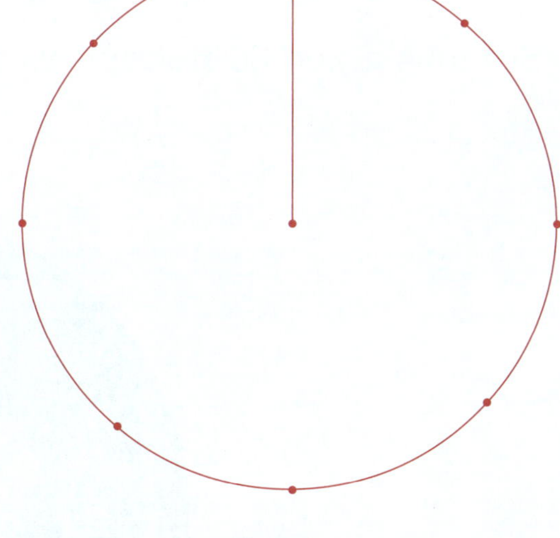

6 Students were asked what game they would like to play during PE. Half the students wanted to play dodgeball. The least popular game was frisbee. The rest wanted to play tag.

Add the labels to this pie chart.

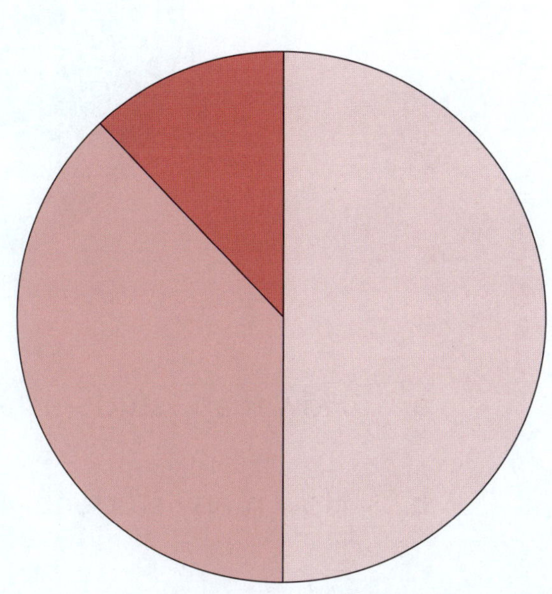

7 A tree is to be planted to mark the school's anniversary. The students voted for which tree they would prefer. The pie graph has been started for you.

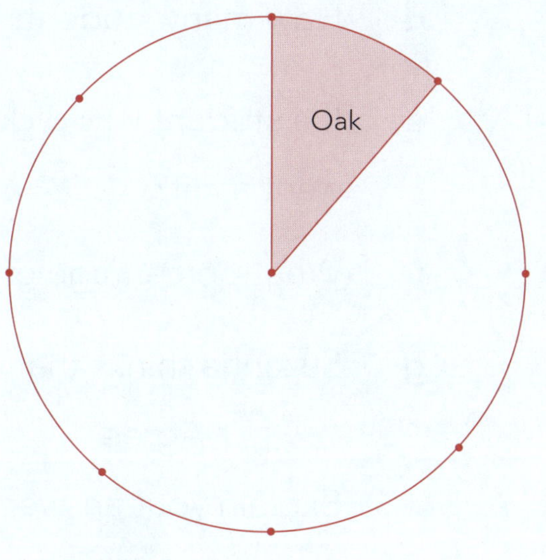

a A quarter wanted a kauri and a quarter wanted a tōtara. Add these sectors to the graph.

b The rest wanted a kahikatea. Label this sector.

c What fraction of the students wanted a kahikatea? ____________

ISBN: 9780170447256

Challenge 2

Suzanna asked 80 students what pet they would like to own.

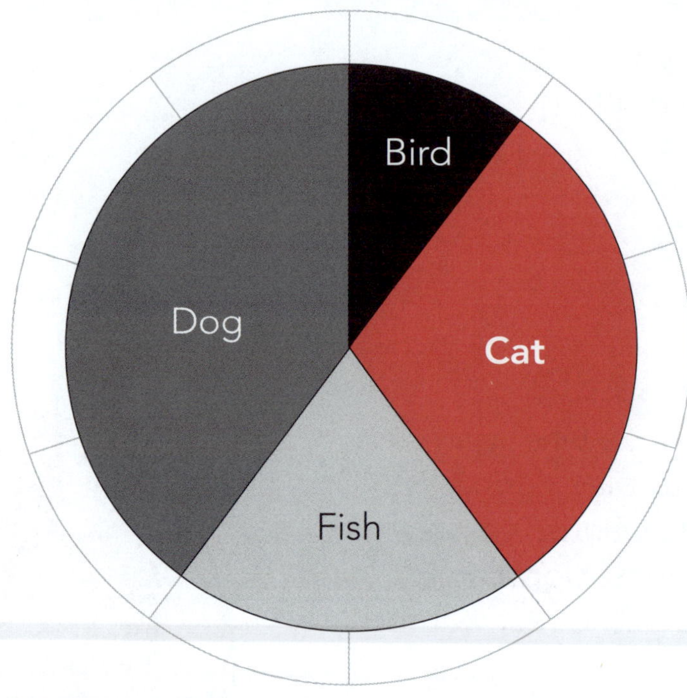

a How many students are represented by each section? ____________

b How many students want to own a fish? ____________

c What was the most popular pet? ____________________

d How many students wanted a bird or a dog? ____________

e If a student was picked at random, what is the probability that they want a cat? ____________

f What percentage of students wanted a bird? ____________

g Suzanna thinks that cats are twice as popular as fish.

☐ Agree ☐ Disagree ☐ Can't tell for sure

Explain your answer. ____

____

 ISBN: 9780170447256

Strip graphs

- Strip graphs can be used with **descriptive** or **discrete** numeric variables.
- They take the form of a rectangular strip which is divided into parts that are different colours or shades.
- The **length** of each part is **proportional to the frequency** of each variable.
- Sometimes they are divided into equal sections, with each section representing the same number of pieces of data.

Understanding strip graphs

Examples:

1 Hair colours were recorded for a group of people.

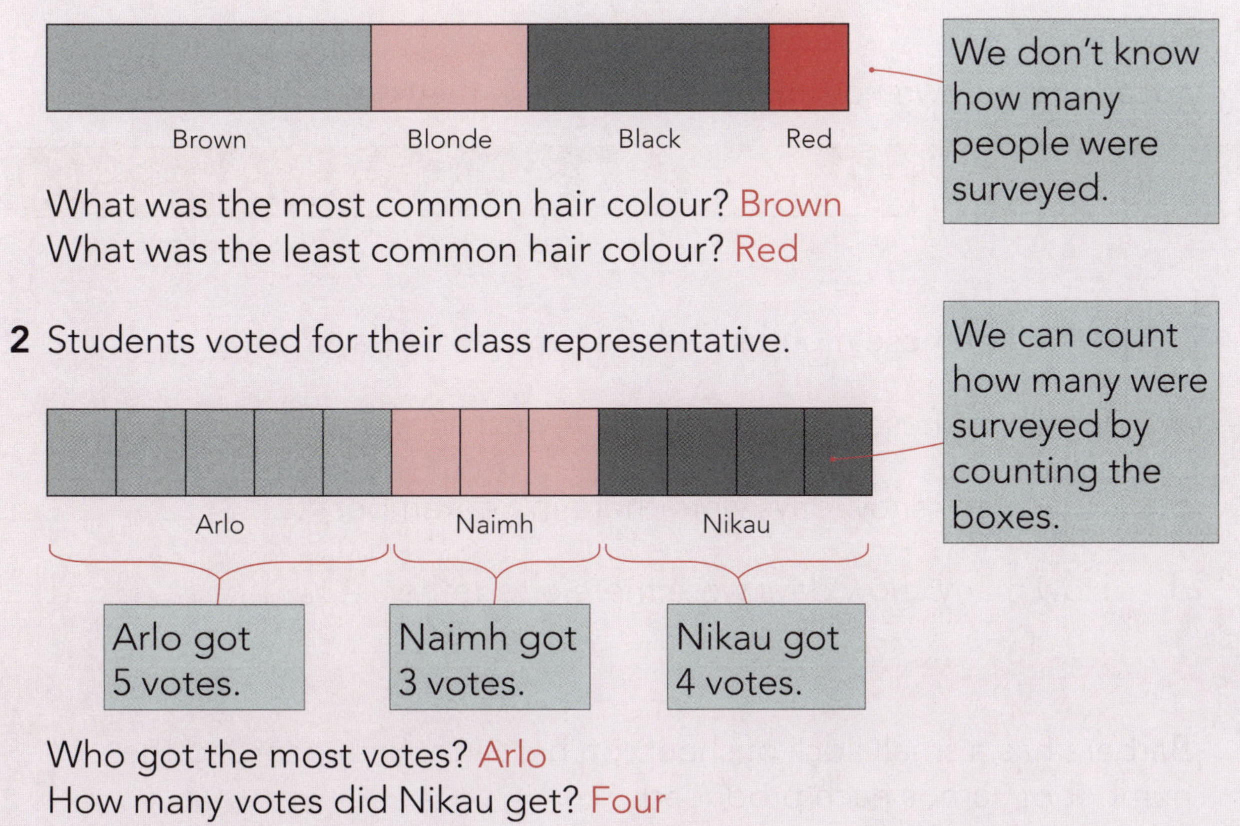

What was the most common hair colour? Brown
What was the least common hair colour? Red

2 Students voted for their class representative.

Who got the most votes? Arlo
How many votes did Nikau get? Four
How many votes were there in total? Twelve

1 Maddison asked her friends what vegetable they disliked eating the most.

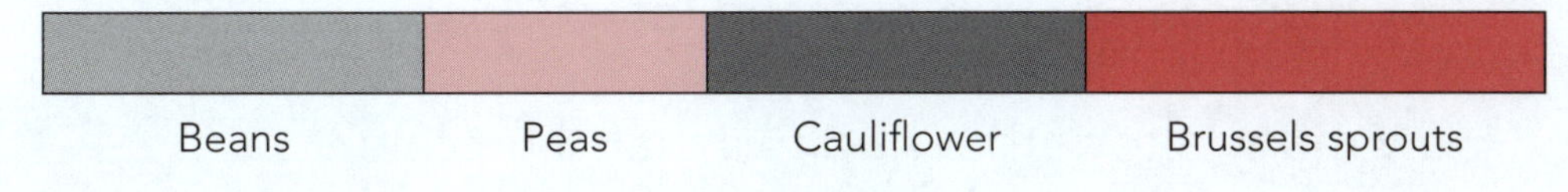

a Which vegetable was the most disliked? ____________________

b Which vegetable was least disliked? ____________________

c Which two vegetables were equally disliked? ____________________

ISBN: 9780170447256

2 Josie orders some plants for her garden.

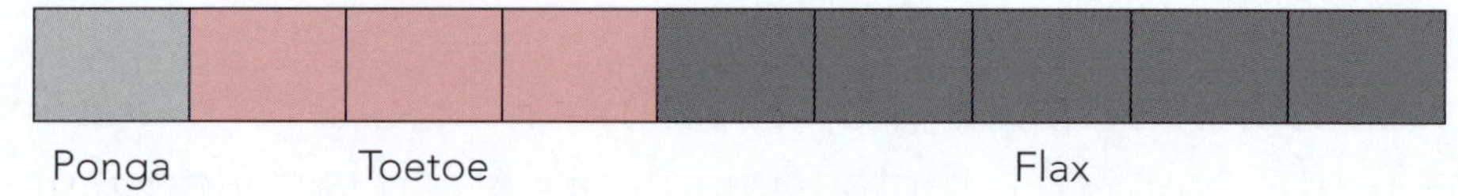

a How many toetoe plants did she order? ____________________

b Which plant does she need only one of? ____________________

c How many plants did she order in total? ____________________

d What fraction of the plants were toetoe? ____________________

3 Lucas wrote down how many days of snow they got each month.

a Which of these months had the most snow days? ____________________

b Which of these months had the fewest snow days? ____________________

c How many snow days were there in September? ____________________

d How many snow days were there altogether? ____________________

4 Barbara has a small flock of sheep on her farm. She recorded the number of lambs each produced.

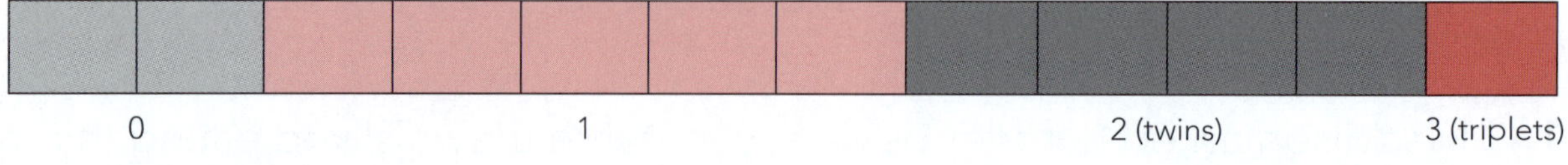

a How many sheep had just one lamb? ____________________

b How many altogether had twins and triplets? ____________________

c What fraction of her flock had twins? ____________________

d How many lambs were born? ____________________

ISBN: 9780170447256

Completing strip graphs

5 Students were asked which musical instrument they would like to learn. The strip graph below has been coloured, but needs labels. Add the labels.
Five students wanted to learn the trumpet, one wanted to learn the flute and the rest wanted to learn the piano.

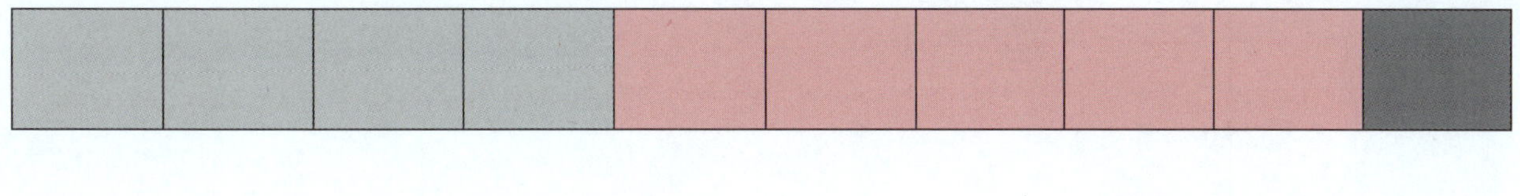

6 Students were asked what card game they would like to play. Add the labels to the strip graph below.
The most popular was snap, the least popular was solitaire. The rest wanted to play rummy.

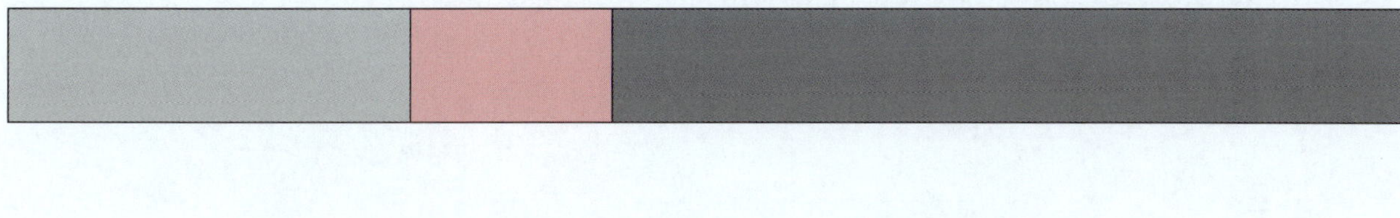

7 Complete this frequency table and then put the information into the strip graph.

Breakfast food	Tally	Frequency
Cereal	𝍸	
Toast	𝍷𝍷	
Eggs	𝍷𝍷𝍷	

Reading axes

- **Axes** are the horizontal and vertical lines which show the scale.
- The **vertical** axis is the **y**-axis, the **horizontal** is the **x**-axis.

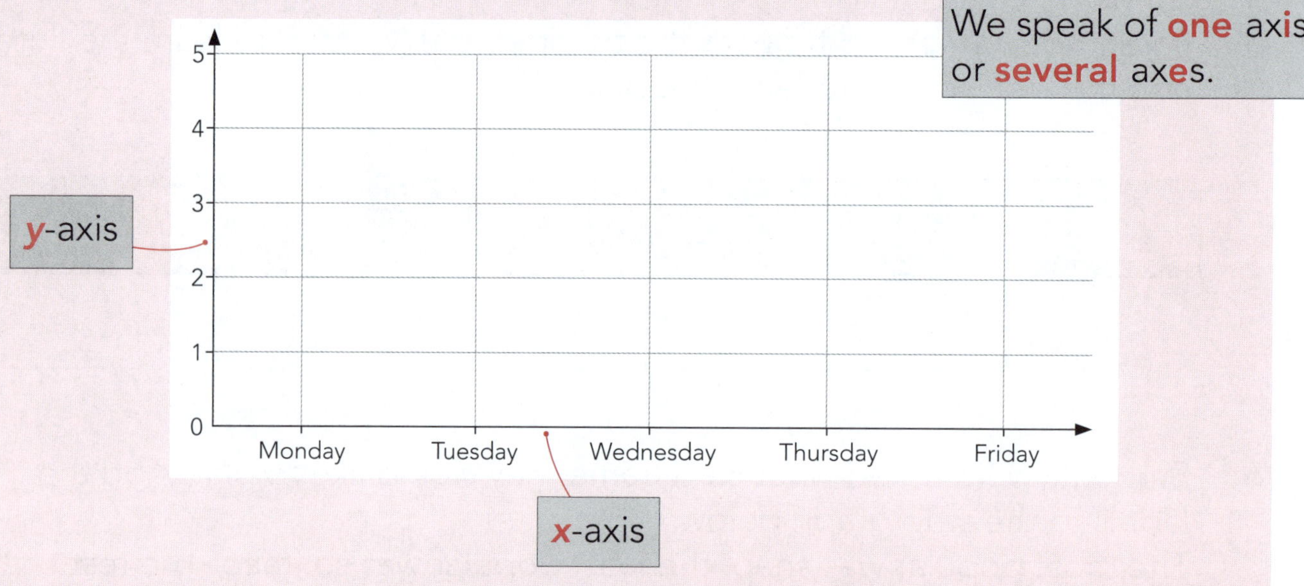

- Sometimes the axes don't increase in ones.
- At times there are major and minor gridlines.

Examples:

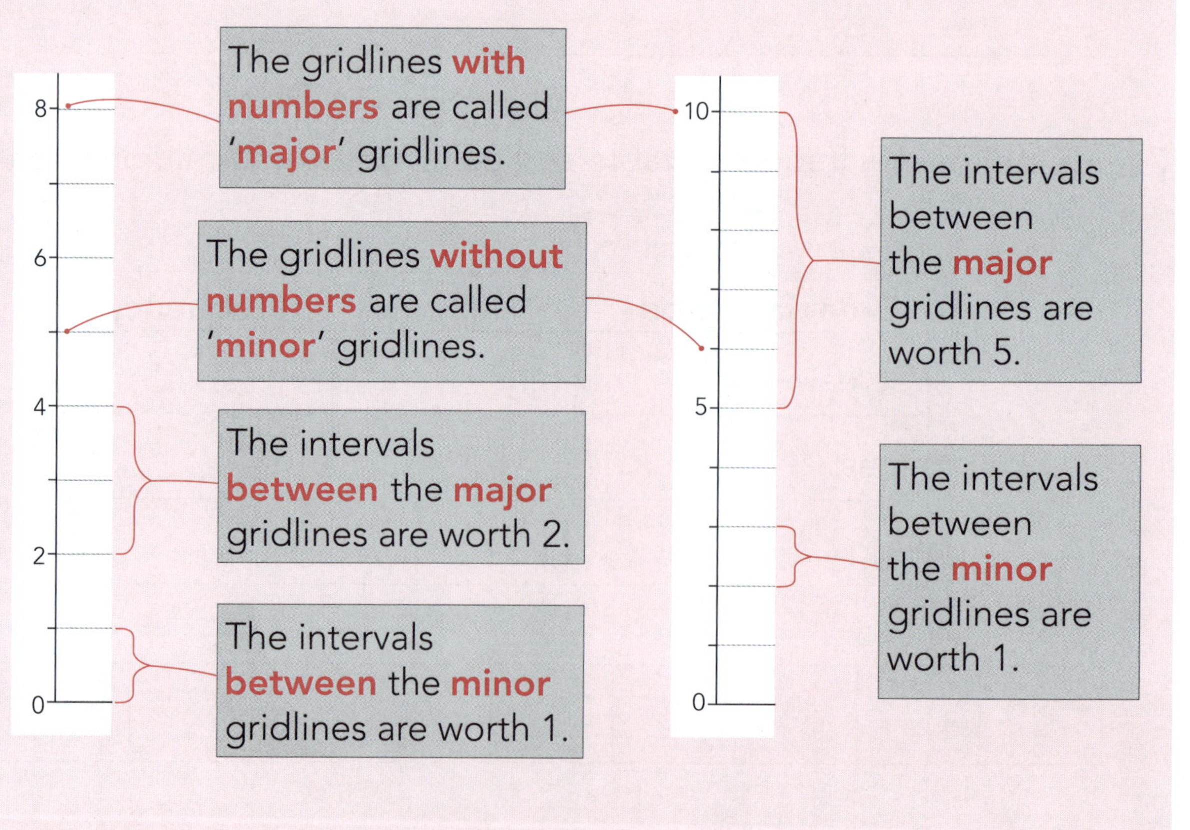

ISBN: 9780170447256

Write down the major and minor intervals, and then fill in the missing values on these axes.

1 Major ______

Minor ______

2 Major ______

Minor ______

3 Major ______

Minor ______

4 Major ______

Minor ______

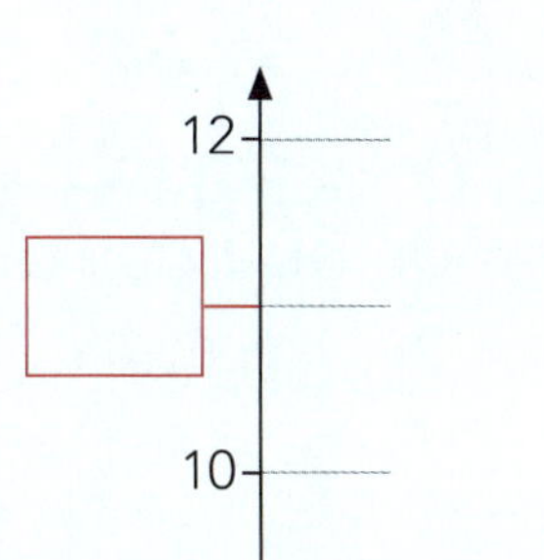

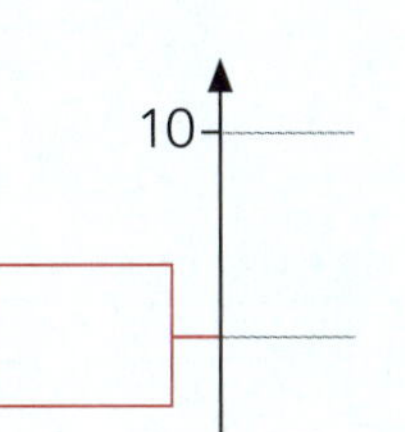

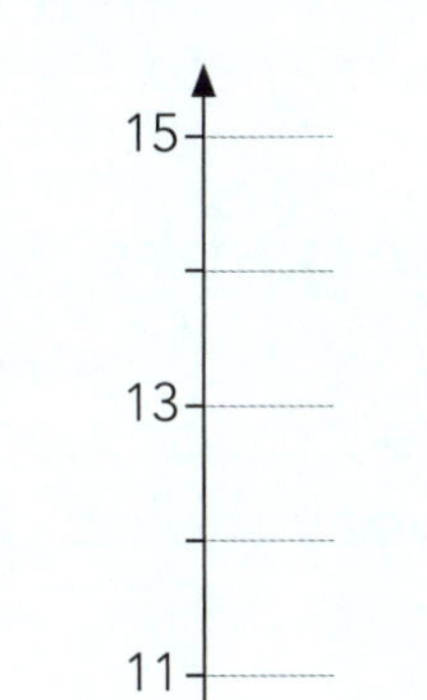

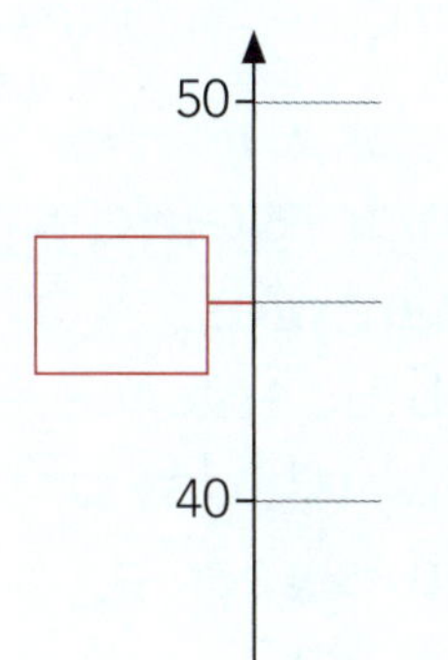

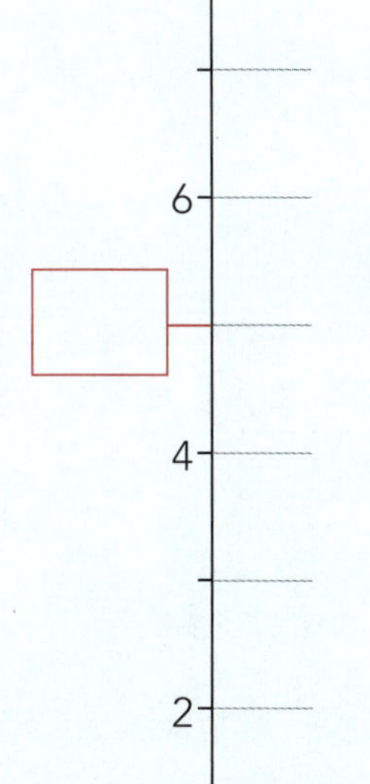

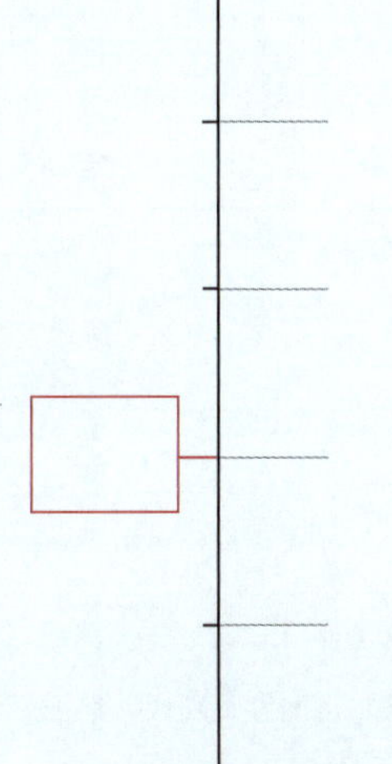

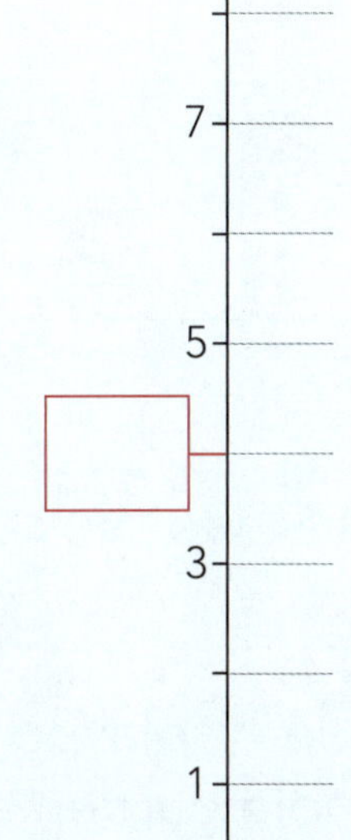

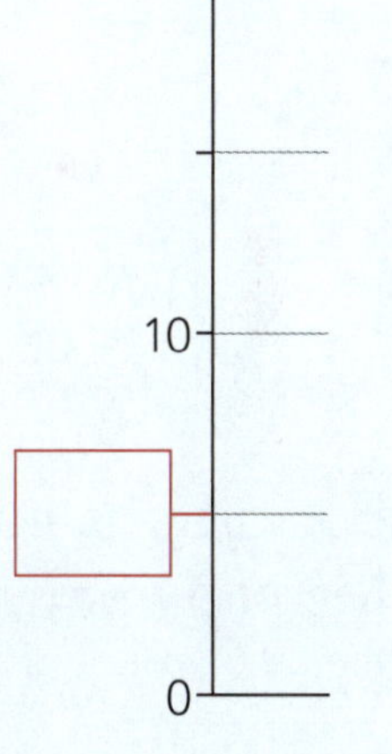

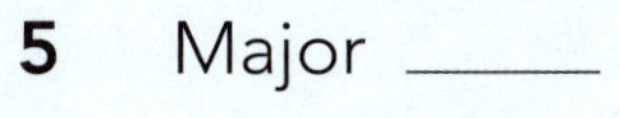

5 Major ______

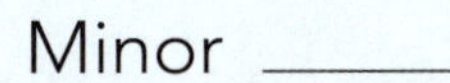

Minor ______

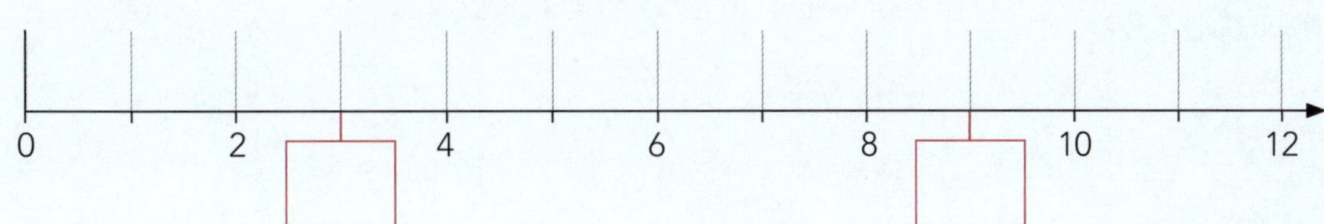

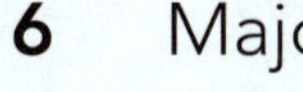

6 Major ______

Minor ______

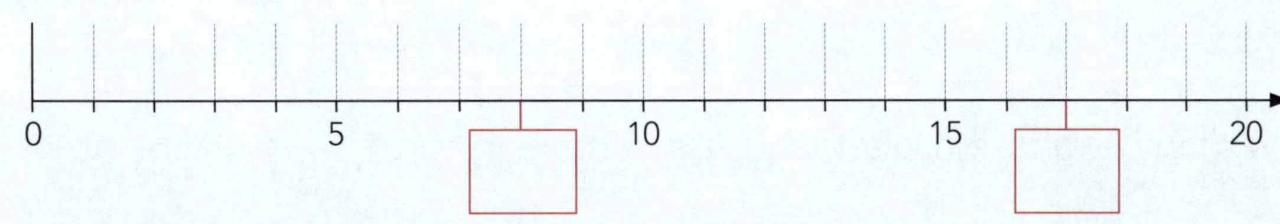

ISBN: 9780170447256

Bar graphs

- Bar graphs are used to display **discrete** or **descriptive** data.
- They are sometimes known as column graphs.
- They can be plotted **vertically** or **horizontally**.
- The bars always have **gaps** between them.

Understanding bar graphs

Examples:

1 Students were asked to look on a calendar to see which day of the week their birthday falls on this year.

Which was the most common birthday day? Saturday, because this is the tallest bar with 10 birthdays.

How many students had birthdays on a Monday? Six, because the bar goes up to 6 on the y-axis.

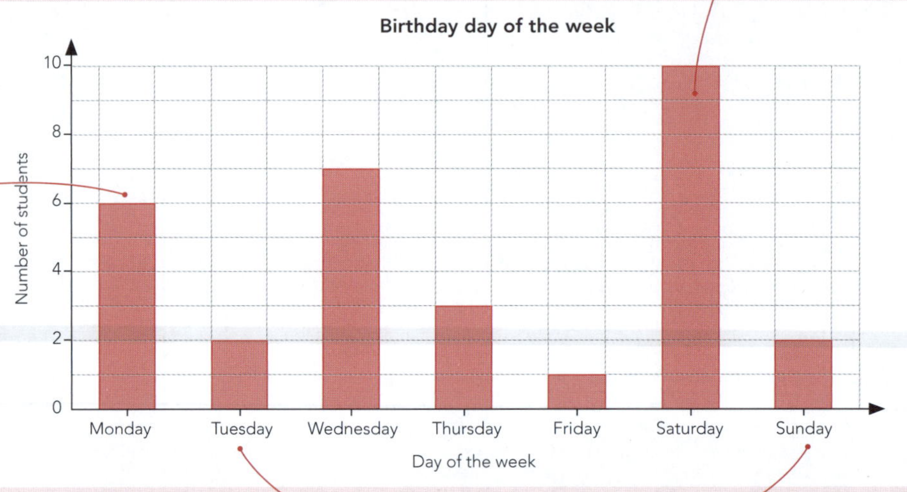

Which two days had the same number of birthdays on them? Tuesday and Sunday, because they both have two birthdays.

2 Bar graphs can also be displayed **horizontally**. The number of plants in Ms Newman's vegetable garden are on this bar graph.

What plant does she have only four of? Lettuce

How many spring onions did she plant? 21

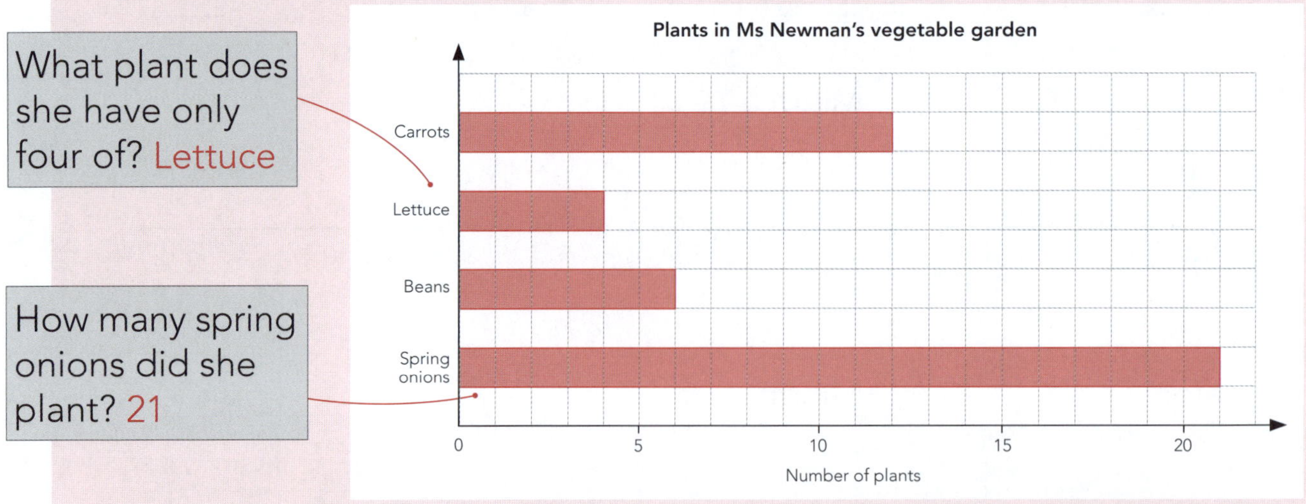

How many vegetable plants does she have in total? $12 + 4 + 6 + 21 = 43$

ISBN: 9780170447256

1 Piri went on a fishing trip with some friends. The bar graph shows their total catch.

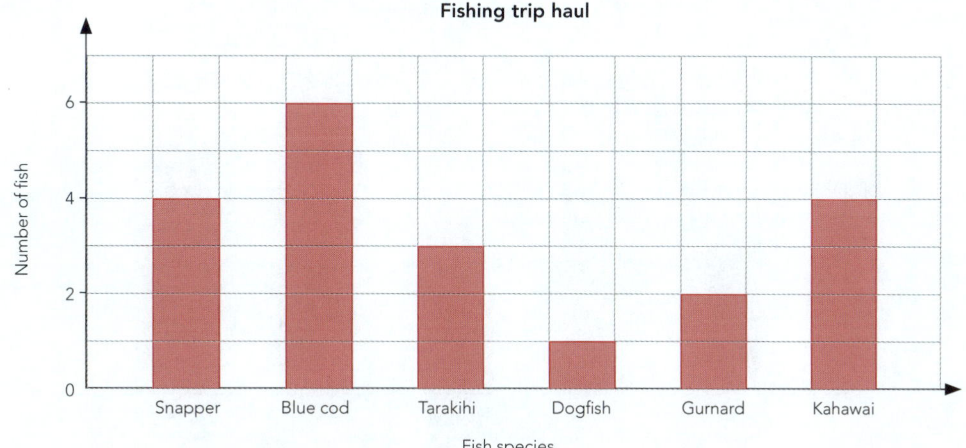

a How many gurnard did they catch? ____________

b What species did they catch the most of? ____________

c Which two species did they catch the same number of? ____________

d How many fish did they catch in total? ____________

2 Kara asked for a summary of the items she had borrowed from her local library over the last six months.

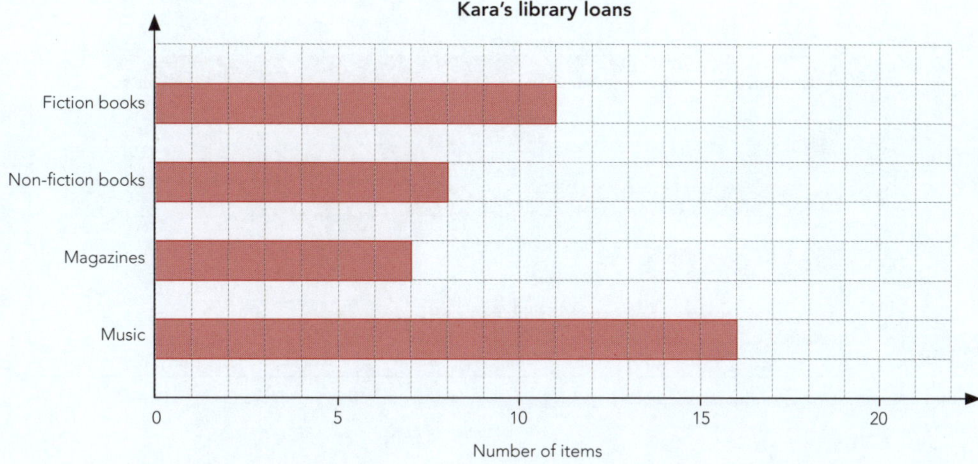

a Which item did she borrow the most of? ____________

b Which item did she borrow the fewest of? ____________

c She borrowed twice as many ____________ as ____________.

3 The bar graph below indicates students' opinions on extending the lunchtime.

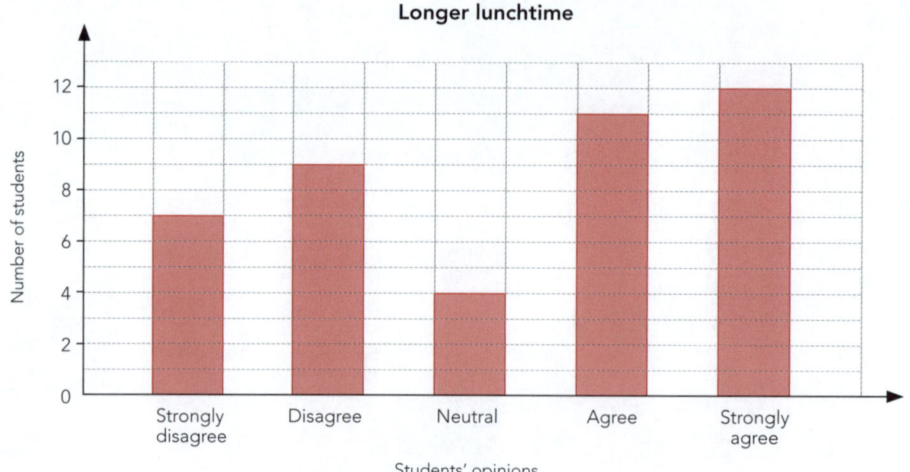

a How many students were neutral? ______

b Which opinion got the most votes? ______

c How many students either disagreed or strongly disagreed? ______

d What fraction of the students either agreed or strongly agreed? ______

4 Manu listed the colours of the neighbourhood cats.

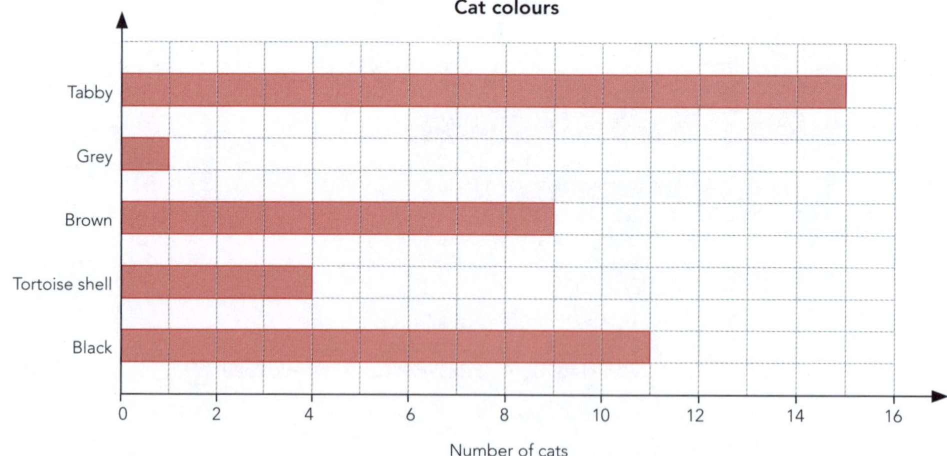

a What was the most common cat colour? ______

b How many cats were not tabby? ______

c How many cats are there in total in Manu's neighbourhood? ______

d What is the probability that the next cat he sees is tabby? ______

 ISBN: 9780170447256

Completing bar graphs

5 Students were offered an item for afternoon tea. This is what they chose. Complete the bar graph.

Afternoon tea	Frequency
Fruit	10
Cheese and crackers	13
Lolly cake	5
Scone	6
Custard square	3
Lamington	17

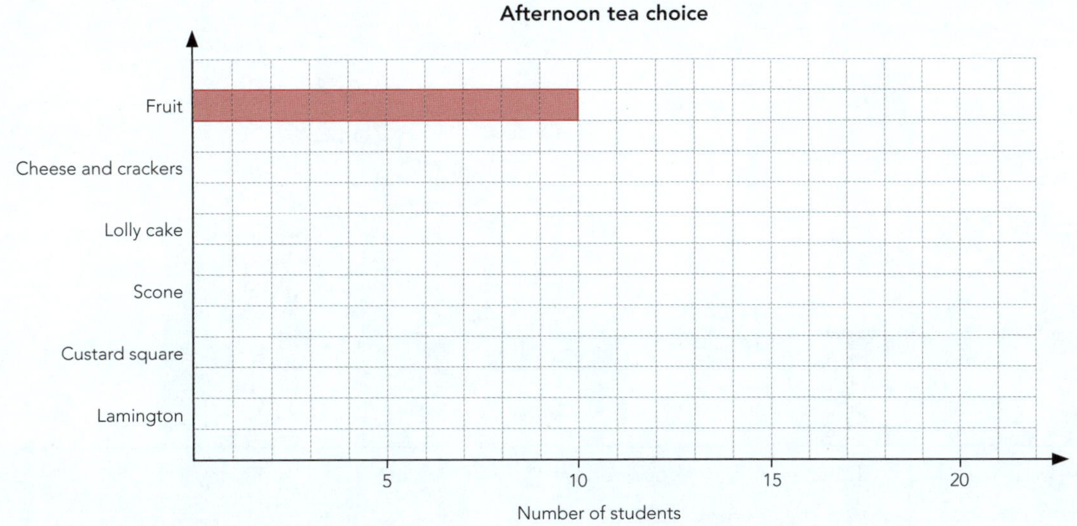

6 Students were asked which music style they prefer to listen to. Complete the frequency chart and bar graph below.

Types of music	Tally	Frequency
Rock	~~IIII~~ I	
Classical	II	
Pop	IIII	
Country	I	
Hip-hop	~~IIII~~ II	

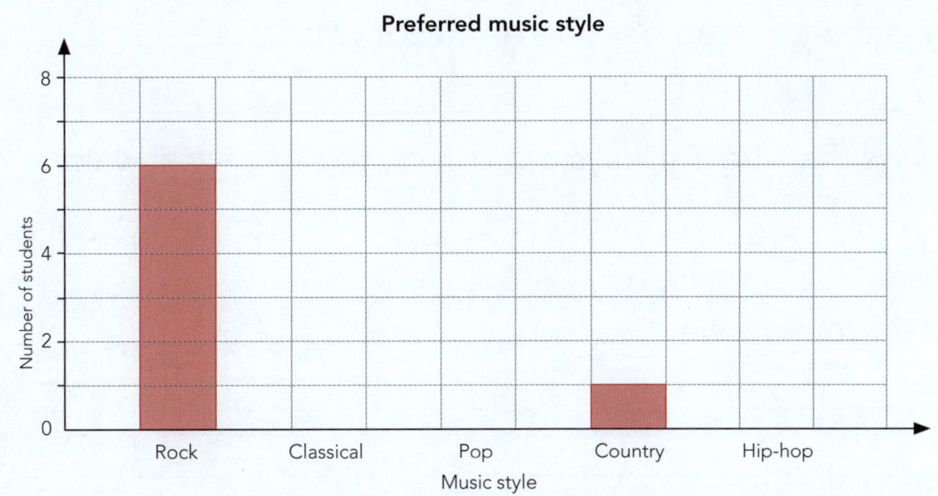

Challenge 3

Every day after school, Kiri goes for a walk.

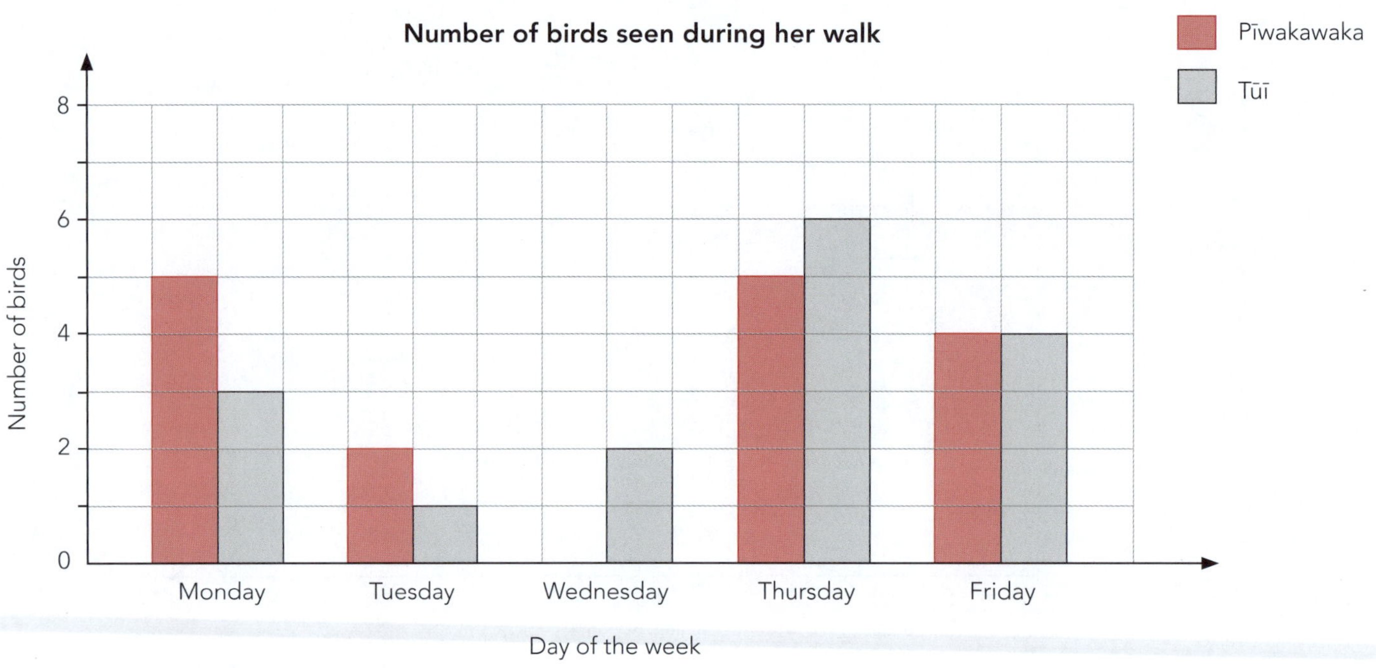

a How many pīwakawaka did she see on Tuesday? ____________________

b How many birds did she see altogether on Thursday? ____________________

c On which day did she see an equal number of tūī and pīwakawaka?

____

d How many tūī did she see in total that week? ____________________

e Why is there no red bar on Wednesday? ____________________

____

f Kiri says that she is always more likely to see pīwakawaka.

☐ Agree ☐ Disagree ☐ Can't tell for sure

Explain your answer. ____________________

____

____

  ISBN: 9780170447256

Line graphs

- Line graphs are often used to show how **discrete** or **continuous** data changes at regular intervals of time.
- Lines connect the plotted points.
- Sometimes these are called **time series** graphs.

Understanding line graphs

Example: Rai recorded the temperature when he got up at 7 a.m each day.

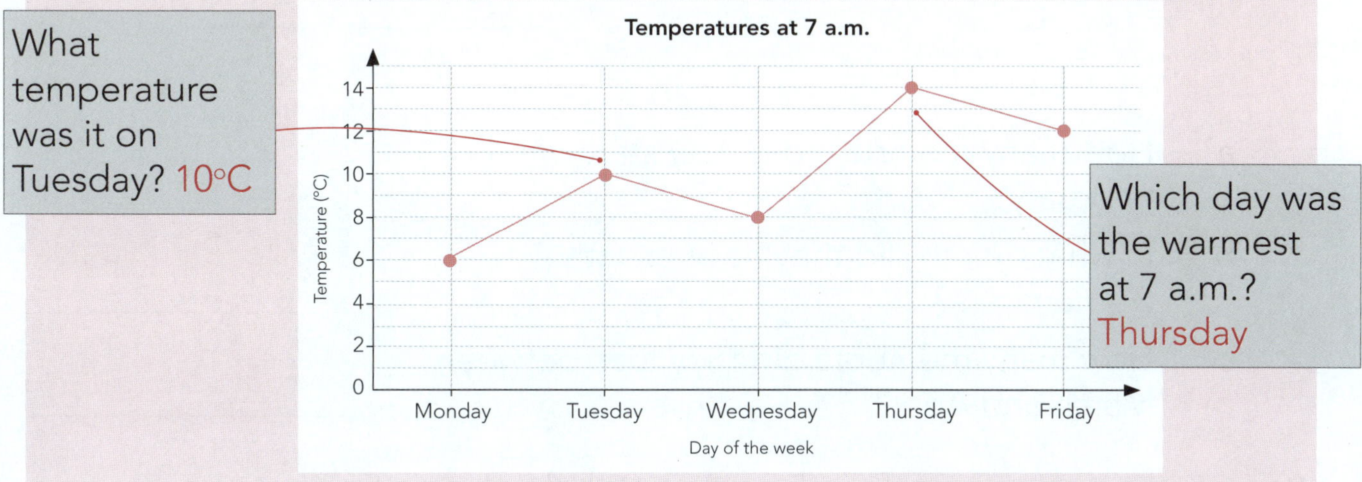

1 The school canteen recorded how many ice blocks it sold over a week.

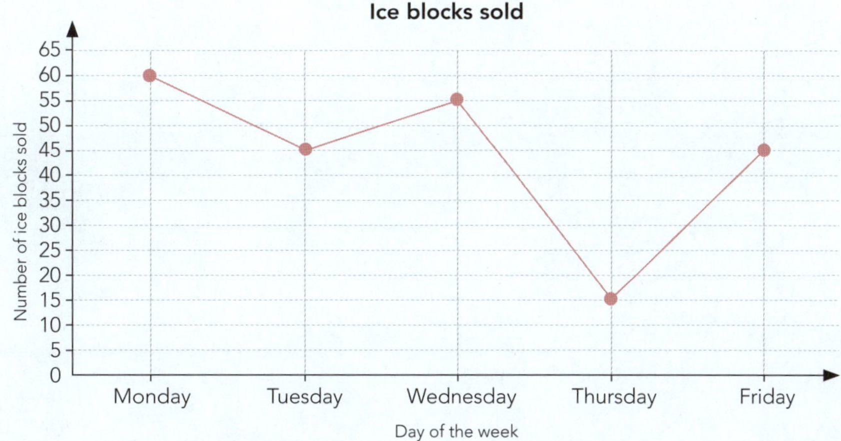

a On which day did they sell the most ice blocks? ________________

b How many ice blocks did they sell on Thursday? ________________

c On which two days did they sell the same number of ice blocks? ________________

2 The Head of Drama recorded the number of members in the drama club through the first half of the year.

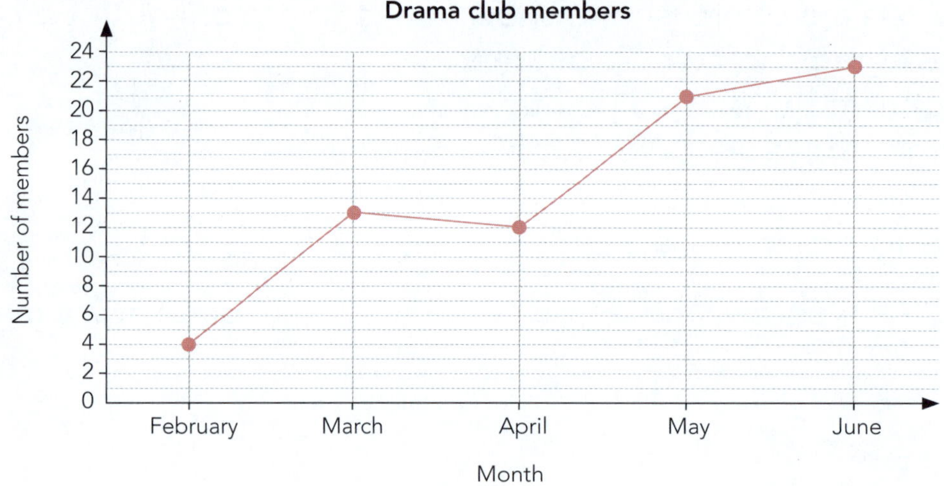

a How many members did they start with in February? ______

b In what month did they have exactly 21 members? ______

c How many members did they lose between March and April? ______

3 Geraldine is training for a 5 km race. She tracks her training runs.

a How long did it take her to run 5 km in week 1? ______

b Geraldine was aiming to do the run in under 45 minutes. In what week did this first happen? ______

c One week she wasn't particularly happy with her time. Which week do you think this was? ______

d Why? ______

ISBN: 9780170447256

Completing line graphs

4 Keziah tracked the height of a bean plant. She plotted the first few days. Complete the line graph for her.

Day	Height (cm)
0	0
2	1
4	4
6	9
8	15
10	21
12	26

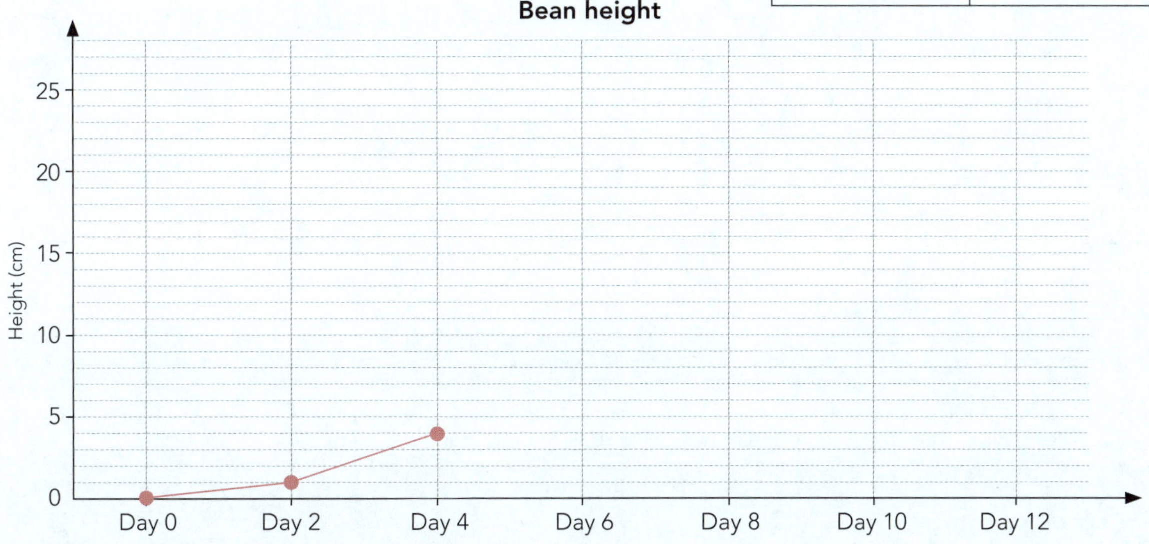

5 Joseph recorded the amount of rain that fell over the week.
Plot the missing points and join them to complete the line graph.

Day	Rain (mm)
Monday	6
Tuesday	14
Wednesday	3
Thursday	0
Friday	8
Saturday	7
Sunday	6

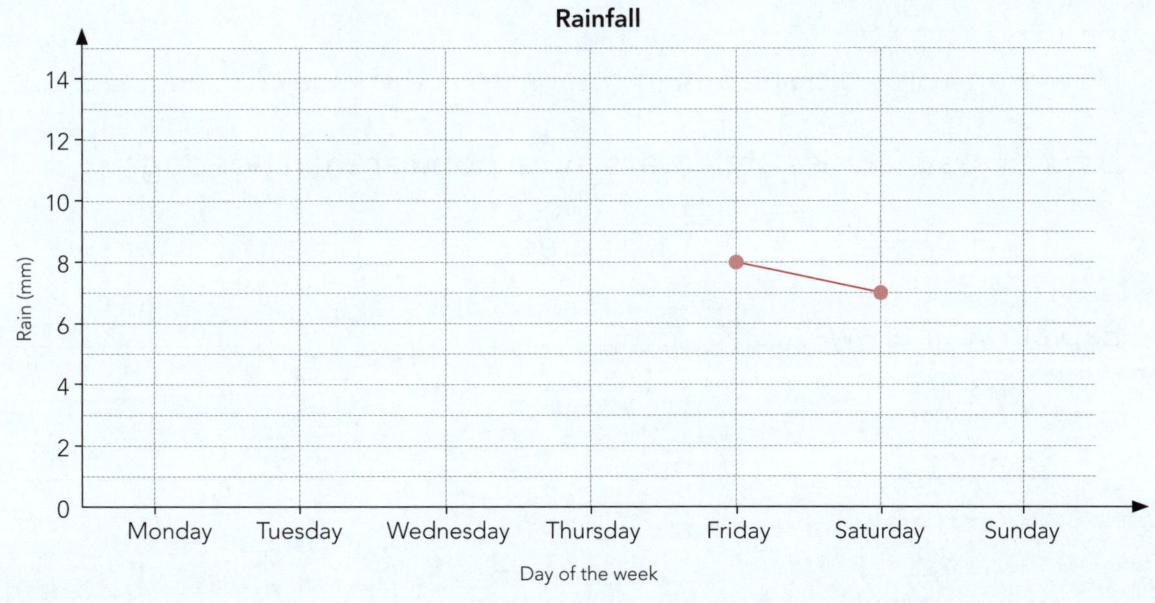

ISBN: 9780170447256

Challenge 4

Luna has a food stall and she kept track of her sales across the week.

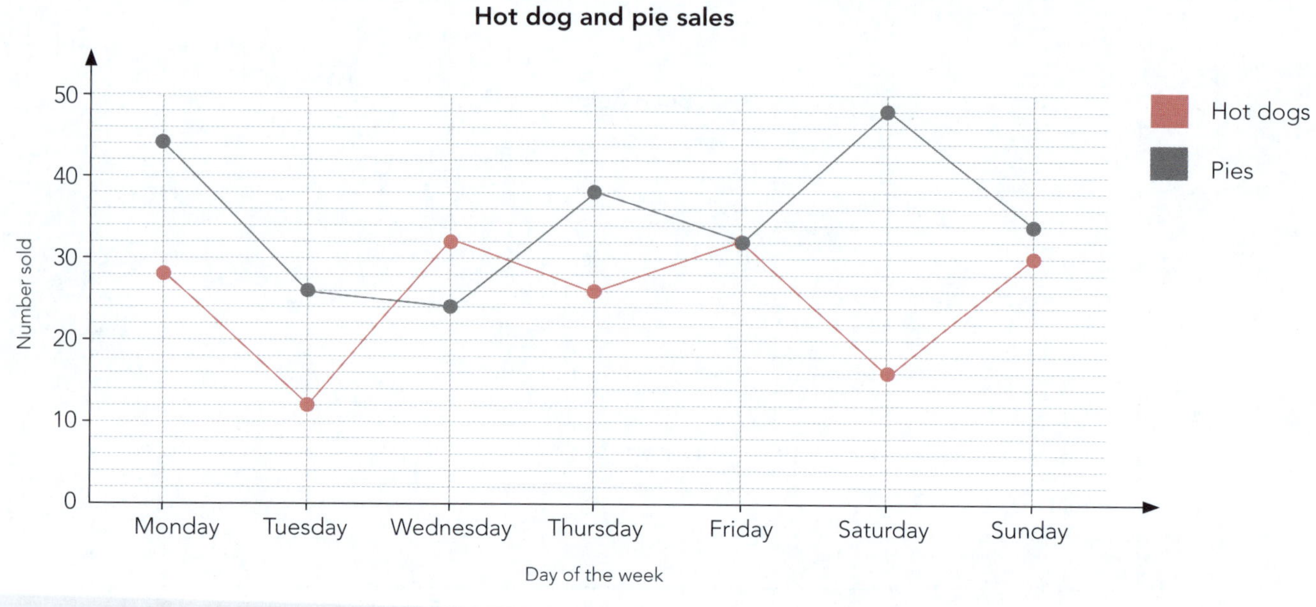

a How many hot dogs did she sell on Saturday? ________________

b On what day did she sell exactly 34 pies? ________________

c What was the day that she sold the least number of hot dogs?

____

d On which day did she sell more hot dogs than pies? ________________

e On which day did she sell the same number of hot dogs as pies?

____

f How many pies did she sell in total across the week? ________________

g Luna thinks that pies are always more popular than hot dogs.

☐ Agree ☐ Disagree ☐ Can't tell for sure

Explain your answer. ________________________________

____

____

ISBN: 9780170447256

Dot plots

- Dot plots are used for **discrete** data.
- They are useful for **comparing groups**.
- Each dot represents one person/object, unless you are told otherwise.

Understanding dot plots

Example: A group of students were asked how many siblings they have.

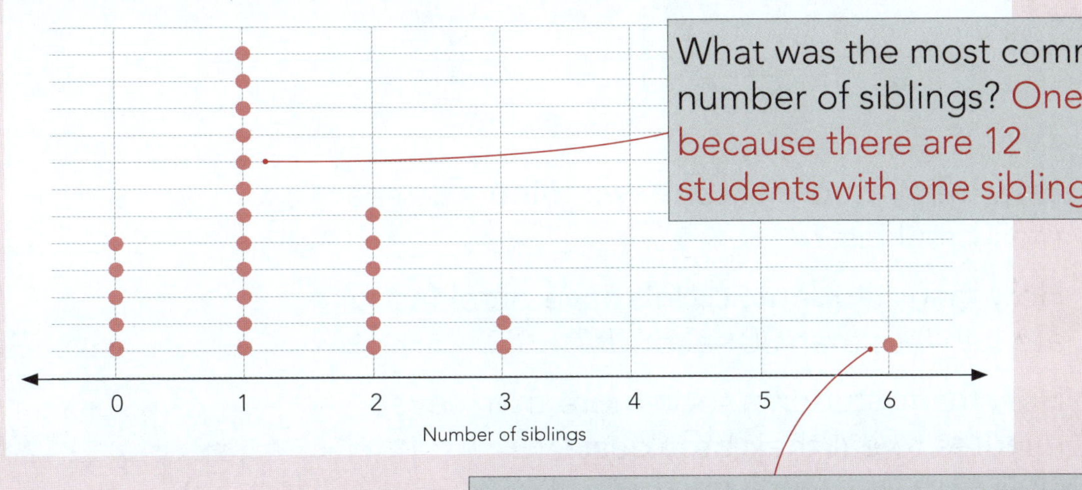

How many students had more than three siblings? Just one, who has six siblings.

How many students were asked? 26, because there are 26 dots.

1 Greg kept a record of how many goals his hockey team scored in each game.

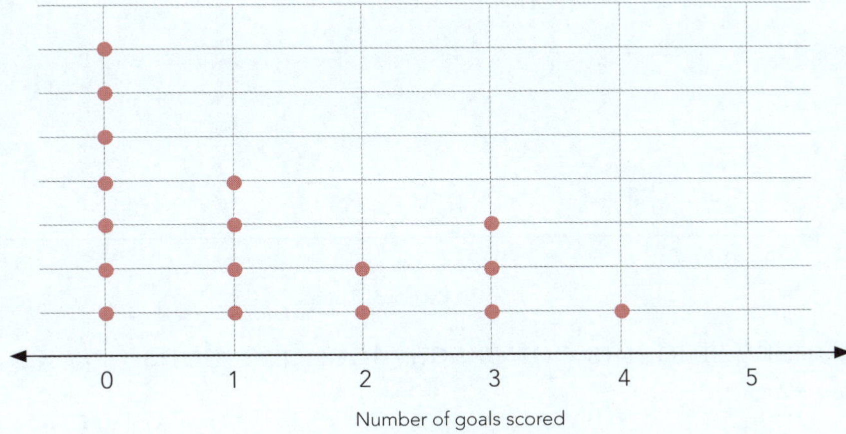

a In how many times did they fail to score any goals? ______________

b How many games did they play in total? ______________

c In how many games did they score at least three goals? ______________

2 Christine asked students to record how long it took them to eat their breakfast in the morning (to the nearest minute).

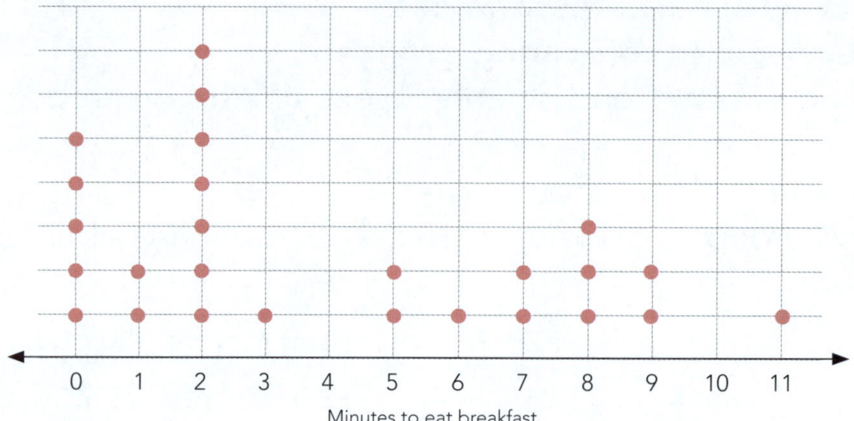

a How many students took two minutes to eat their breakfast? ____________

b How many students didn't have breakfast or ate it in less than 30 seconds? ____________

c How many students took more than seven minutes to eat their breakfast? ____________

d What fraction of the students took at least nine minutes to eat their breakfast? ____________

3 A quiz was given to a class. Their results are shown below.

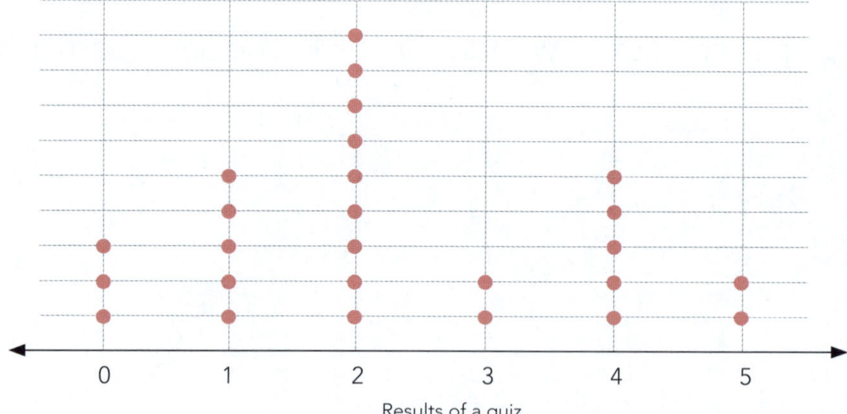

a How many students got exactly four questions correct? ____________

b What was the highest score? ____________

c How many students got fewer than two questions correct? ____________

d What is the probability that a student got exactly two correct answers? ____________

  ISBN: 9780170447256

Completing dot plots

4 Riley asked his friends to record the time it took to brush their teeth, to the nearest minute. The results are in the table. Add the data from the bottom row of the table to the dot plot.

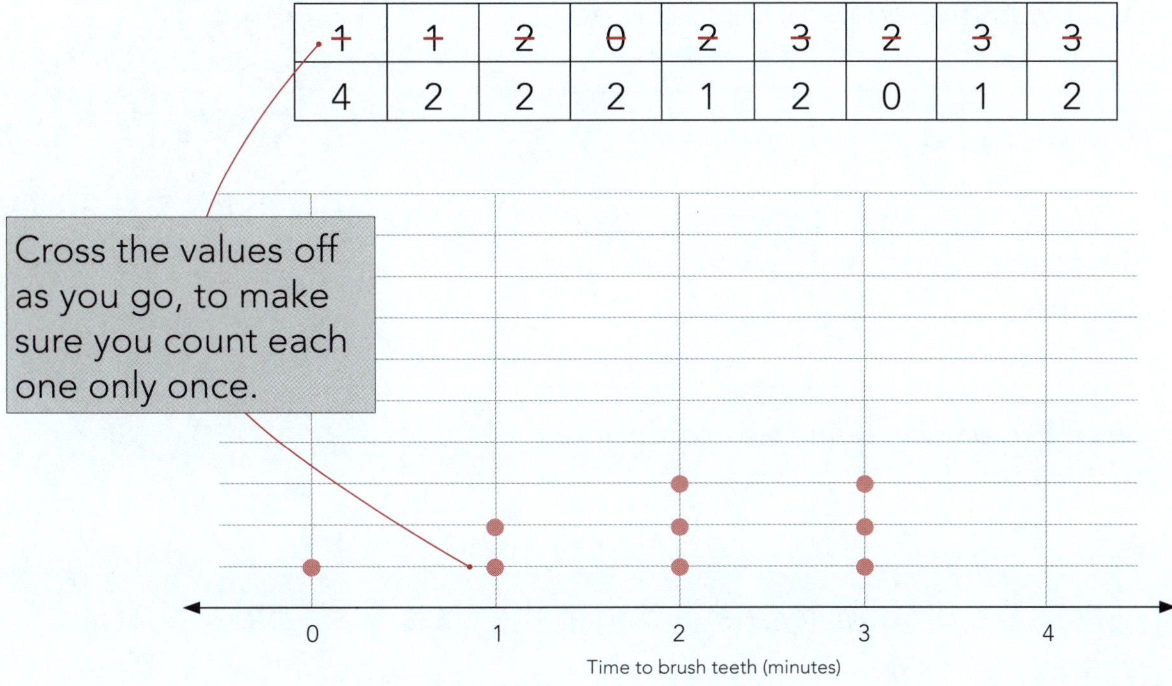

~~1~~	~~1~~	~~2~~	~~0~~	~~2~~	~~3~~	~~2~~	~~3~~	~~3~~
4	2	2	2	1	2	0	1	2

5 Kaia surveyed some students about how many detentions they have had at school. Complete the dot plot of this information.

~~0~~	~~0~~	~~1~~	~~2~~	~~0~~	0	0	4	3	0	2
1	2	3	0	0	4	1	1	2	2	1

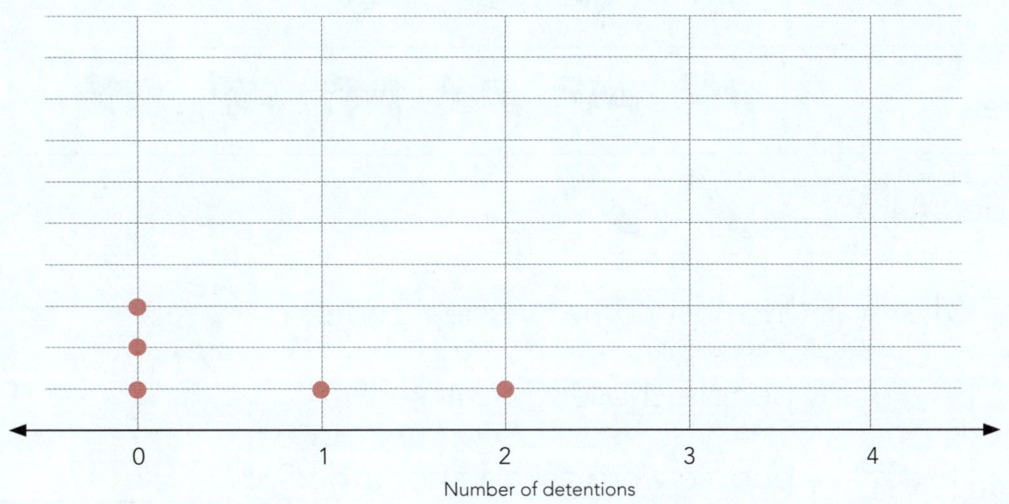

Mixing it up

1 Hattie took her dog to puppy classes and recorded the breeds of all the dogs.

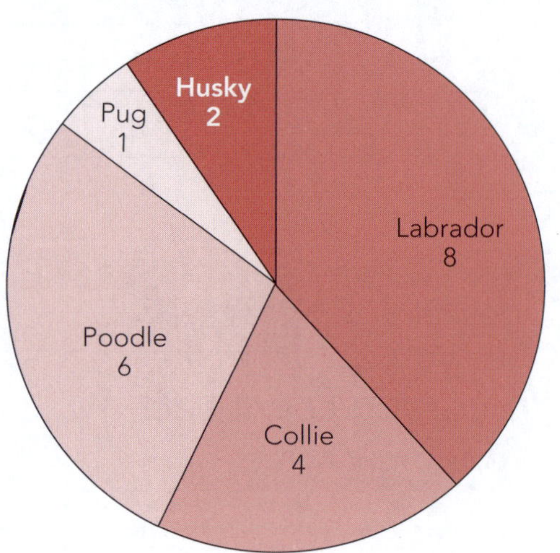

a What was the most common breed?

____

b How many poodles were there?

____

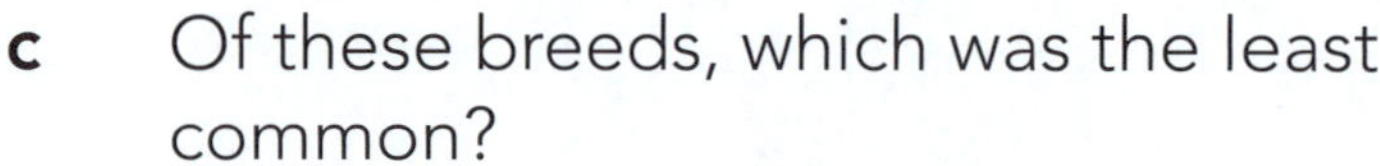

c Of these breeds, which was the least common?

____

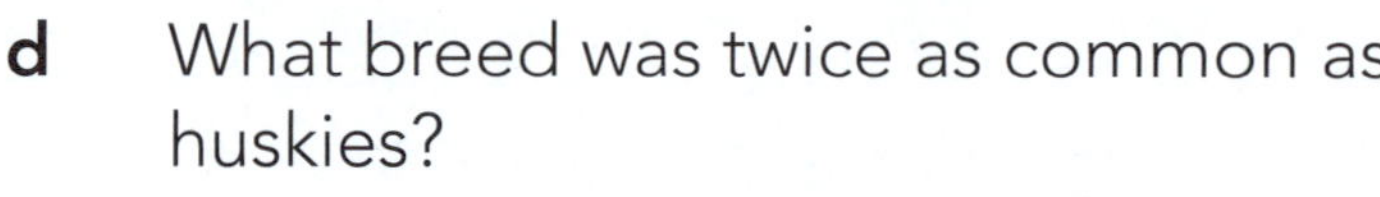

d What breed was twice as common as huskies?

____

e What is the probability that a dog in the class was a breed that started with 'P'? _______________________

2 Wedding guests were asked what they would like for their meal. This pictogram shows their choices.

Meal choice	
Fish	
Chicken	
Beef	
Vegetarian	

a What was the most common meal choice? _______________

b How many people chose the chicken? _______________

c How many people were asked altogether? _______________

d What percentage of people chose fish? _______________

 ISBN: 9780170447256

3 Roberto asked people to write down the number of days in a week that they do exercise.

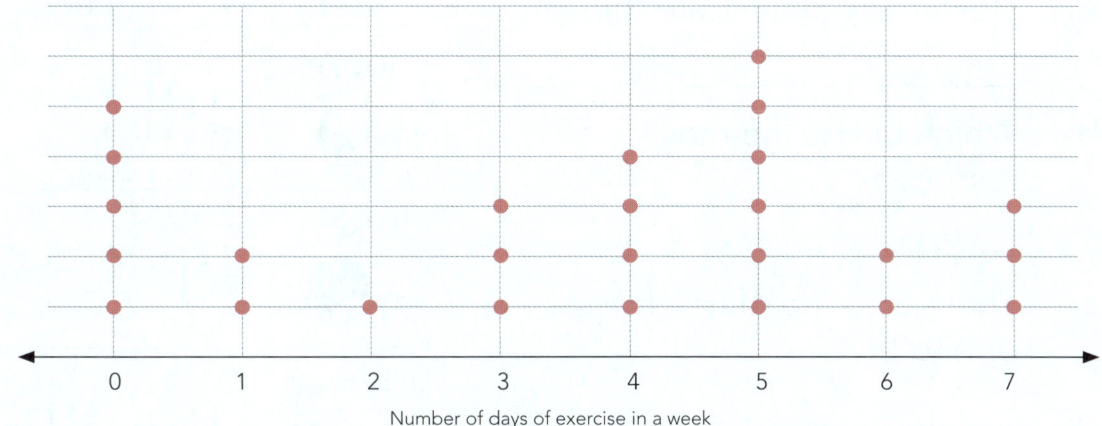

a How many people exercise every day of the week? ____________

b How many people don't exercise any days of the week? ____________

c What was the most common number of days a week to exercise? ____________

d What fraction of people exercised fewer than three days a week? ____________

4 Luke has a small orchard with a variety of fruit trees.

a What fruit trees does he have the most of? ____________

b How many plum trees does he have? ____________

c What fruit tree does he have the smallest number of? ____________

d How many more nectarine trees than apricot trees does he have? ____________

5 The table shows the poultry that Sam has on his block of land.

a How many turkeys are there?

____

b Which bird is the most common?

____

c There are nine of which type of bird?

____

d How many birds are on his block?

____

Item	Tally
Goose	𝍸 |
Turkey	|||
Chicken	𝍸 𝍸 ||
Duck	𝍸 ||||

6 The local gym tracked its membership numbers for the last half of the year.

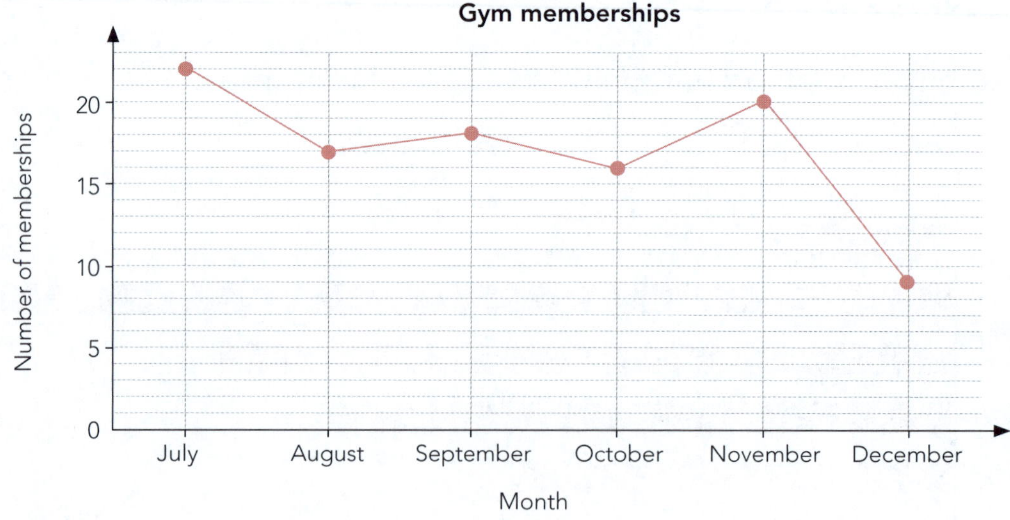

a How many members did they have in September? ______________

b What was the highest number of members? ______________

c How many new members did they get between October and November? ______________

d How much did their membership drop by over the six months? ______________

 ISBN: 9780170447256

7 Peter collected information about students' most disliked house chore.

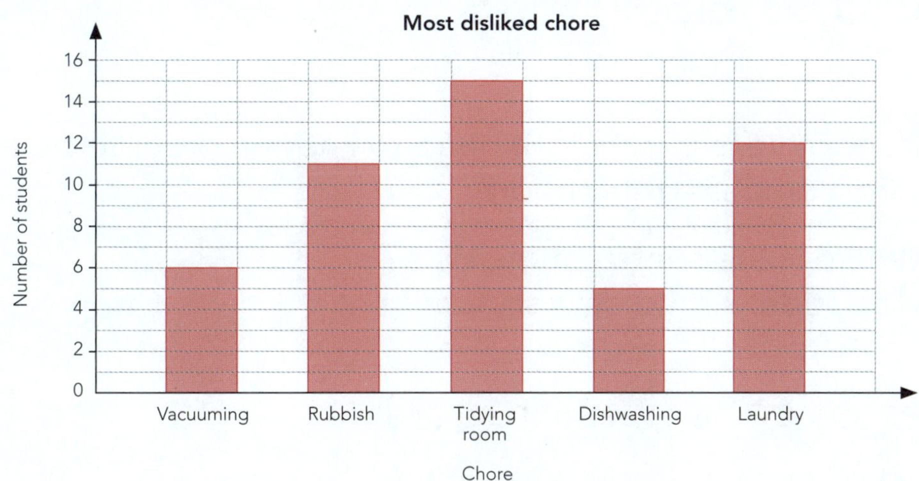

a How many students disliked dishwashing the most? __________

b What was the most disliked chore? __________

c What chore was twice as disliked as vacuuming? __________

d How many more students disliked laundry than rubbish? __________

e What fraction of the students disliked rubbish the most? __________

8 Maria watched the traffic go past her classroom and noted the type of vehicle.

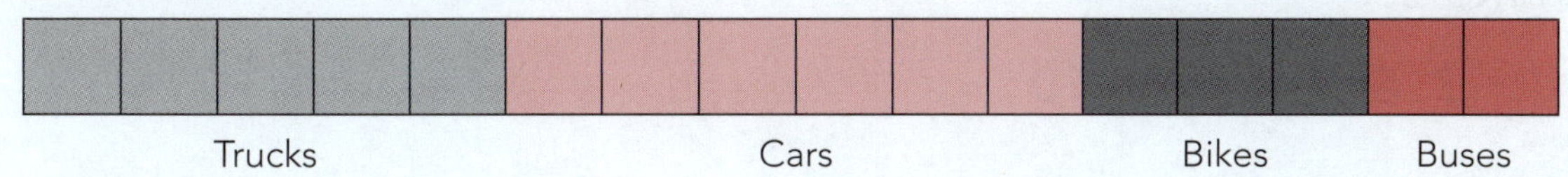

a What was the most common type of vehicle? __________

b How many trucks went past? __________

c __________ were twice as likely to go past as __________.

d How many vehicles went past in total? __________

e What percentage of the vehicles were buses? __________

ISBN: 9780170447256

Data analysis

- There are two measures that we need to know in order to be able to discuss and compare distributions:

  1 Where is the **centre** of the data?
  2 How widely is the data **spread**?

Measures of centre (averages)

- There are **three** measures for the centre of the data.

Name	Calculation
Mean	$\frac{\text{the sum of all the data values}}{\text{the number of data values}}$
Median	middle value
Mode	value that occurs most frequently

Mean

- The mean is sometimes falsely called the average.
- The numbers do not need to be in order for this calculation.
- Means are often long decimals, so sensible rounding may be needed.

$$\textbf{mean} = \frac{\textbf{sum of all the data values}}{\textbf{number of data values}}$$

Examples:

1 3 8 1 4 7 9 10

$$\text{Mean} = \frac{3 + 8 + 1 + 4 + 7 + 9 + 10}{7}$$
$$= 6$$

There are 7 numbers in the data set.

The mean of this data set is 6.

2 11 0 4 3 7 5 0

$$\text{Mean} = \frac{11 + 0 + 4 + 3 + 7 + 5 + 0}{7}$$
$$= 4.2857...$$

Round to 4.3.

Notice that 0 must be included in the calculation.

The mean of this data set is 4.3.

 ISBN: 9780170447256

1 Calculate the means of these data sets.

a **4 9 3 6 1 7** Mean = $\frac{4 + 9 + 3 + 6 + 1 + 7}{6}$ = ______

b **1 7 3 2 5 8 10 12** Mean = $\frac{1 + \quad}{8}$ = ______

c **9 5 0 3 7 1 5 6 2 7** Mean = $\frac{\quad}{10}$ = ______

d **5 3 6 5 5 12 16 0** Mean = ______ = ______

e **21 26 22 27 29 23** Mean = ______ = ______

Median

- Before you can calculate the median, you must **put the data in order**.

Median with an odd data set

- If there is an **odd number of values** in a data, the median is the **middle number**.

Examples:

1

1 3 5 7 8 9 10 12 14

~~1~~ 3 5 7 8 9 10 12 ~~14~~

~~1~~ ~~3~~ 5 7 8 9 10 ~~12~~ ~~14~~

~~1~~ ~~3~~ ~~5~~ 7 8 9 ~~10~~ ~~12~~ ~~14~~

~~1~~ ~~3~~ ~~5~~ ~~7~~ 8 ~~9~~ ~~10~~ ~~12~~ ~~14~~

Cross off one number from each end until you get to the middle number.

Four numbers. This is the **middle** number. Four numbers.

The median of this data set = 8.

2

1 1 2 2 3 3 5 7 9 9 9

Five numbers. Five numbers.

The median of this data set = 3.

3 0 2 4 5 6 **6** 6 7 8 10 12

Zero counts as a number.

This is the **middle** number.

The median of this data set = 6.

2 Find the medians of these data sets.

a 1 4 7 9 12 Median = ____________

b 2 2 4 5 6 7 7 8 10 Median = ____________

c 1 2 3 3 3 3 4 5 6 7 8 Median = ____________

d 0 0 2 3 4 4 5 6 7 7 9 11 12 Median = ____________

e 0 0 0 1 1 1 1 2 2 2 3 3 3 Median = ____________

Median with an even data set

- If there is an **even number of values**, the median is **halfway between the two middle numbers** in the data set.

Examples:

1 2 3 4 **5** **7** 8 9 12

These are the middle numbers. Add them together and divide by 2.

The median of this data set $= \frac{5+7}{2} = 6$.

2 4 5 6 8 **9** **9** 10 12 14 15

The two middle numbers are both 9.

The median of this data set = 9.

3 3 5 6 8 **10** **22** 26 27 28 30

There could be a large gap between the two middle values.

The median of this data set $= \frac{10+22}{2} = 16$.

 ISBN: 9780170447256

3 Find the median of these data sets.

a **1 3 6 8 9 10** Median = $\frac{6 +}{2}$ = ______

b **2 3 5 6 6 8 10 16** Median = $\frac{+}{2}$ = ______

c **2 2 5 6 8 12 12 14 15 18** Median = $\frac{+}{2}$ = ______

d **0 0 0 1 1 2 4 4 4 6 6 6** Median = $\frac{+}{}$ = ______

e **0 1 3 4 6 7 9 10 11 11 12 29** Median = ______ = ______

Median when the numbers are out of order

- Before you can calculate the median, you must **put the data in order**.

Example:

~~6~~ ~~3~~ ~~7~~ ~~1~~ ~~2~~ ~~6~~ ~~3~~ ~~8~~ ~~5~~

Cross the numbers off as you go to make sure you don't miss any.

Put them **in order** before finding the median.

1 2 3 3 5 6 6 7 8

Check you have the same number of pieces of data.

The median for this data set is 5.

4 Put these data sets in order and then find the median.

a **~~1~~ 3 7 ~~2~~ 9 5 3 6**

1 2 ______________________ Median = ______

b **0 12 3 5 8 1 2 4 5 15**

______________________ Median = ______

c 5 2 1 8 4 4 2 1 0

____________________ Median = ________

d 15 1 17 22 9 7 8 19

____________________ Median = ________

e 1 5 19 2 9 17 6 1 0

____________________ Median = ________

Mode

- The mode is the **most common value**.
- Sometimes there are **several modes**.
- If there are **three or more** numbers that occur equally often, we say there is **no mode**.

Examples:

1 9 5 8 (4) 1 2 7 (4)

The most common number in this data set is **4**: there are two of them.

The mode of this data set is 4.

2 (8) 6 3 (8) (9) 1 (8) (9) 2 1 (9)

Both **8** and **9** occur three times.

The modes are 8 and 9.

3 (2) (1) (7) (2) 9 6 (7) (1)

There are three numbers that occur equally often: **1**, **2** and **7**.

There is no mode.

If there are **three or more** 'modes', we say there is **no mode** at all.

 PHOTOCOPYING OF THIS PAGE IS RESTRICTED UNDER LAW. ISBN: 9780170447256

5 Find the modes of these data sets.

a 2 3 3 4 5 7 7 7 9 Mode = ______________

b 9 0 1 5 3 9 7 2 9 1 Mode = ______________

c 12 16 19 17 15 13 12 Mode = ______________

d 8 5 3 2 5 7 4 6 2 1 6 3 Mode = ______________

e 8 8 3 2 8 3 2 2 8 8 2 3 2 Mode = ______________

6 Match the data sets to their mode.

9 2 1 3 5 7 8 0 3 4 •	• No mode
Mode = 1 •	• 7 4 0 3 2 1 0 5 4 0
7 5 1 0 3 2 4 2 3 4 •	• 4 4 1 1 4 1 4 1 1
No mode •	• Modes = 2 and 3
5 3 6 7 2 2 1 2 3 7 •	• Mode = 3
4 3 5 2 2 6 7 2 3 8 3 •	• 4 0 3 1 1 2 3 2 8 0
Mode = 0 •	• Mode = 2

ISBN: 9780170447256

Measure of spread — range

Range

- The range is calculated by finding the biggest number (maximum) in a data set and subtracting the smallest number (minimum) in the data set.
- Note: the range is a **single number**.
- Like the mean, the range is affected by any unusually big or small values.
- The data does not need to be ordered to calculate the range. However it can be useful to do so.
- The range is a measure of the **variability** of the data.

Range = maximum – minimum

Example:

5 9 6 3 7 4 12 10 7 4

The **biggest** value in the data set (**maximum**).

The **smallest** value in the data set (**minimum**).

Range = 12 – 3
= 9

The range or the spread of this data set is 9.

1 Calculate the range for the following data sets.

a **2 3 4 4 5 8 9** Range = 9 – ______ = ____________

b **9 14 7 3 8 12 11 9** Range = ______ – ______ = ____________

c **8 4 2 6 4 7 4 5 1** Range = ______ – ______ = ____________

d **15 13 18 12 10 20 15** Range = ____________ = ____________

e **1 9 19 9 1 91 19 9** Range = ____________ = ____________

f **16 18 45 38 95 101 34** Range = ____________ = ____________

g If the biggest number in a data set is 17 and the range is 11, what's the smallest value? ____________________

ISBN: 9780170447256

Putting it together

Calculate the mean, median, mode and range of these data sets.

1 **1 2 2 6 7 7 8 9 12**

Mean = ______________________________ = ________

Median = __________ Mode = ____________ Range = ___________

2 **3 5 5 6 9 11 11 13**

Mean = ______________________________ = ________

Median = __________ Mode = ____________ Range = ___________

3 **7 0 9 6 2 1 5 4 2** ________________________________

Put the numbers in order.

Mean = ______________________________ = ________

Median = __________ Mode = ____________ Range = ___________

4 **12 6 4 8 3 9 5 1 11 18** ________________________________

Mean = ______________________________ = ________

Median = __________ Mode = ____________ Range = ___________

ISBN: 9780170447256

5

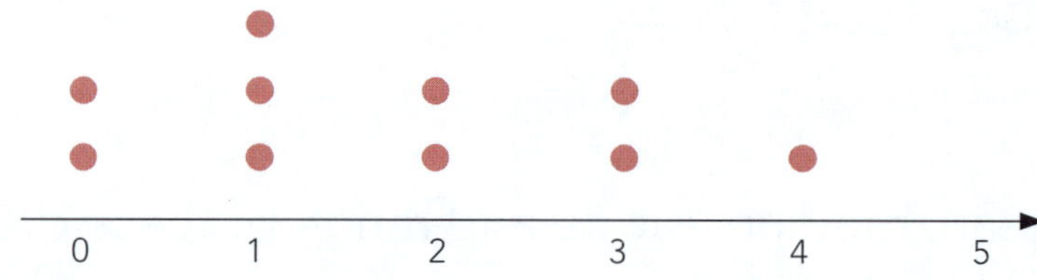

a List the data: ______________________________

b Find the following.

Mean = ______________________________ = __________

Median = __________ Mode = __________ Range = __________

6

a List the data: ______________________________

b Find the following.

Mean = ______________________________ = __________

Median = __________ Mode = __________ Range = __________

7

a List the data: ______________________________

b Find the following.

Mean = ______________________________ = __________

Median = __________ Mode = __________ Range = __________

 ISBN: 9780170447256

8 The graph shows the number of goals scored in a series of hockey games.

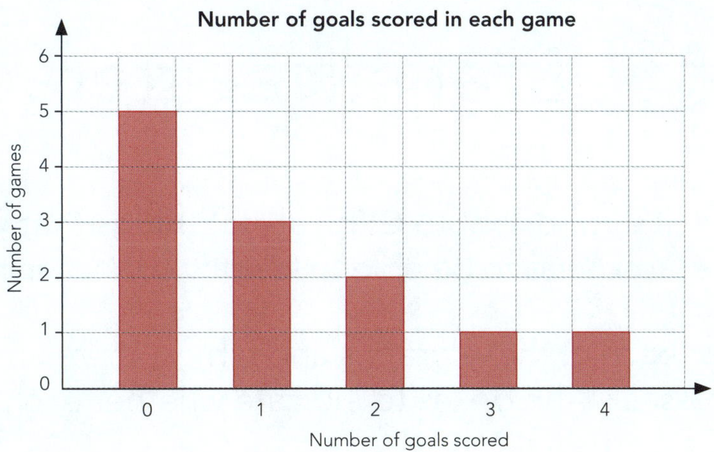

a List the number of goals scored in each game:

____

b Find the following.

Mean = ______________________________ = __________

Median = __________ Mode = __________ Range = __________

9 Tui has 15 goats. She has recorded the number of kids each goat has produced.

a List the number of kids produced by each goat:

____

b Find the following.

Mean = ______________________________ = __________

Median = __________ Mode = __________ Range = __________

ISBN: 9780170447256

Statistical literacy

- It's important to **think** about things that you see and read.
- You need to be able to identify correct and incorrect conclusions from data.

For each of these graphs and tables, there are several statements. Put ticks or crosses in the boxes to indicate whether each is a correct interpretation or not.

1 Students wrote down which animal they were most afraid of.

Item	Tally
	卌 II
	卌 卌 IIII
	卌 III
	卌

a Most students were afraid of animals with legs. 

b Fourteen students were most afraid of sharks. 

c Equal numbers of students were most afraid of rats and spiders. 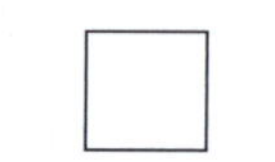

2 Mei and Evie recorded their results from the 'Ten quick questions' at the start of each of 13 lessons.

a Mei got twice as many 7s as 8s. 

b It could be argued that Evie did better because her median is one more than Mei's. 

c Evie's results were more variable than Mei's. ☐

d It could be argued that Mei did better because she got 10 three times. ☐

 ISBN: 9780170447256

3 'The New Zealand flag should be changed.' Thirty-five students wrote down their opinions about this statement.

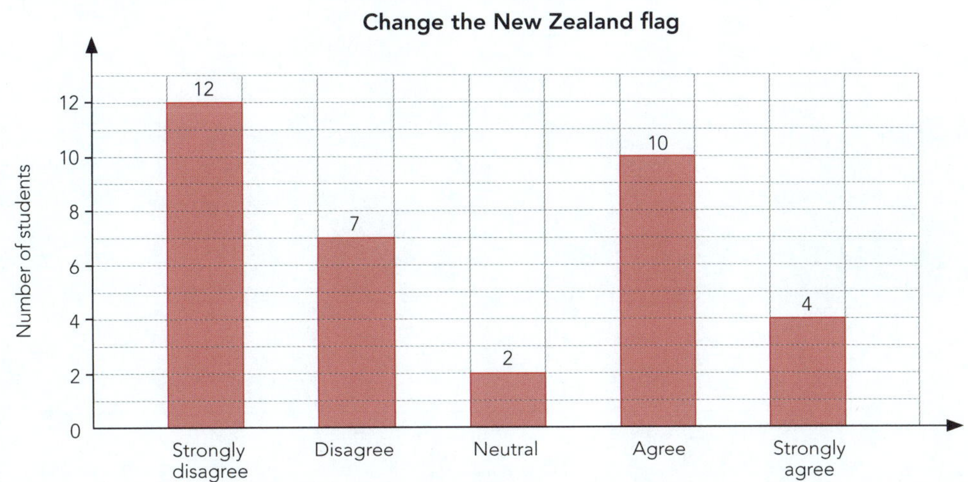

a Most students either disagreed or strongly disagreed. ☐

b Most students thought the flag should be changed. ☐

c More than half the students had strong opinions about this issue. ☐

4 Students going to camp were asked to write down their favourite spread.

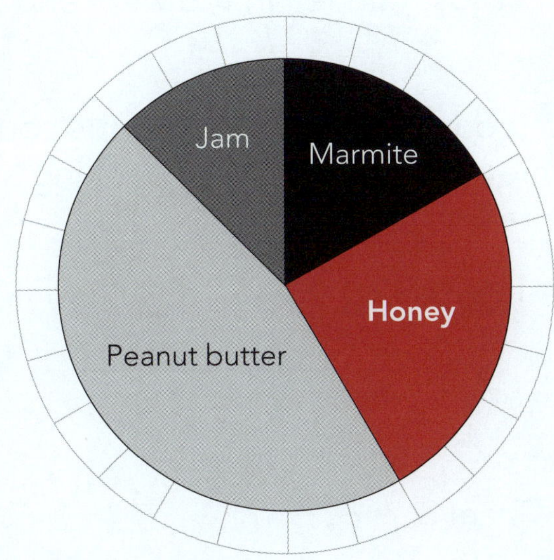

a More than half preferred peanut butter. ☐

b Honey was twice as popular as jam. ☐

c Most students preferred honey, Marmite or jam. ☐

d More students preferred honey or Marmite to peanut butter. ☐

ISBN: 9780170447256

5 Heidi recorded the rainfall every day while they were at camp.

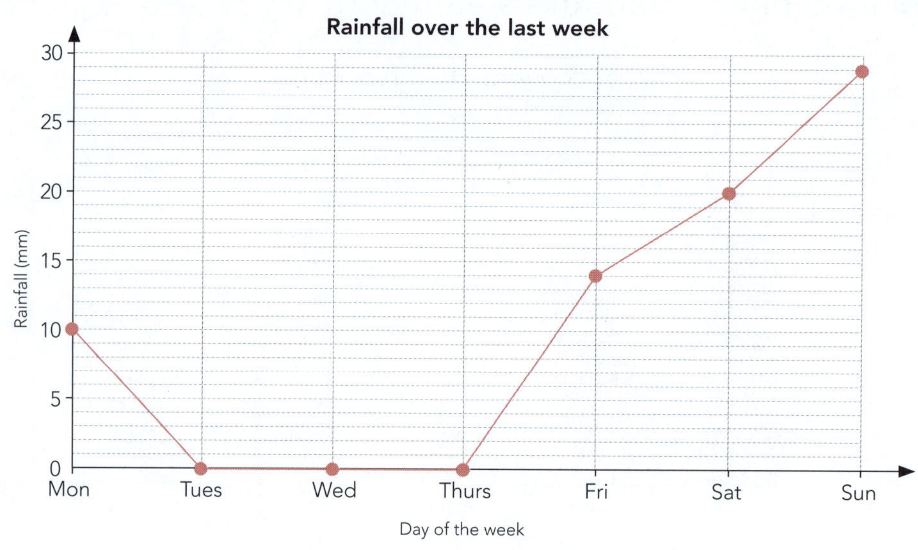

a Twice as much rain fell on Monday than on Saturday. ☐

b On Saturday there was 6 mm more rain than on Friday. ☐

c It will rain next Friday. ☐

d Most rain fell in the weekend. ☐

6 Each day during camp, groups could earn points based on teamwork, achievements, quality of cooking and cleaning, etc. Here are the results for teams A and B.

Team A

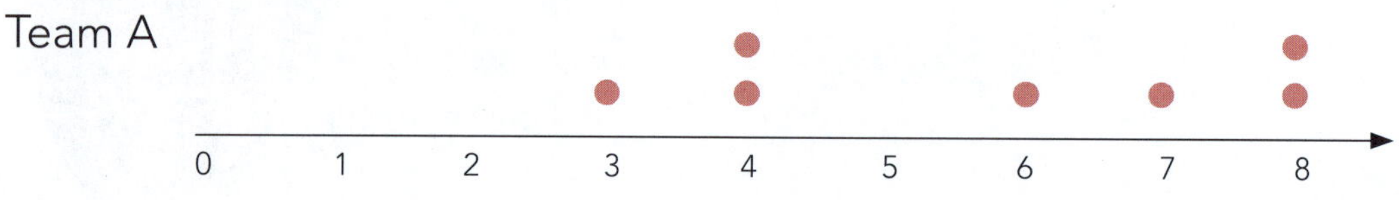

Team B

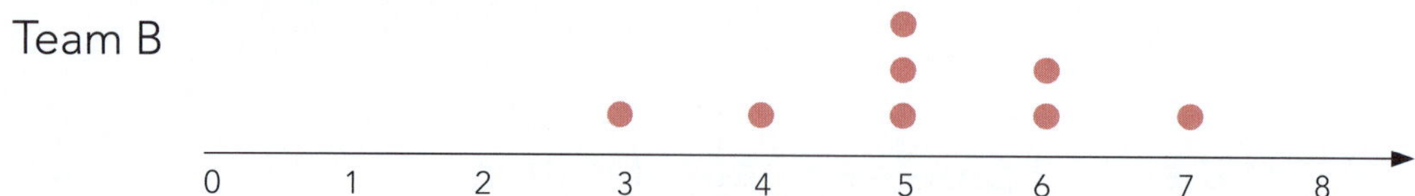

a Team A was more consistent than team B. ☐

b The median for team A is higher than the median for team B, so it could be argued that team A did better. ☐

c Team B got more points in total, so it could be argued that team B did better. ☐

 ISBN: 9780170447256

7 Toby's mum measured his height on every birthday. Put ticks or crosses in the boxes to indicate whether each statement is correct or not.

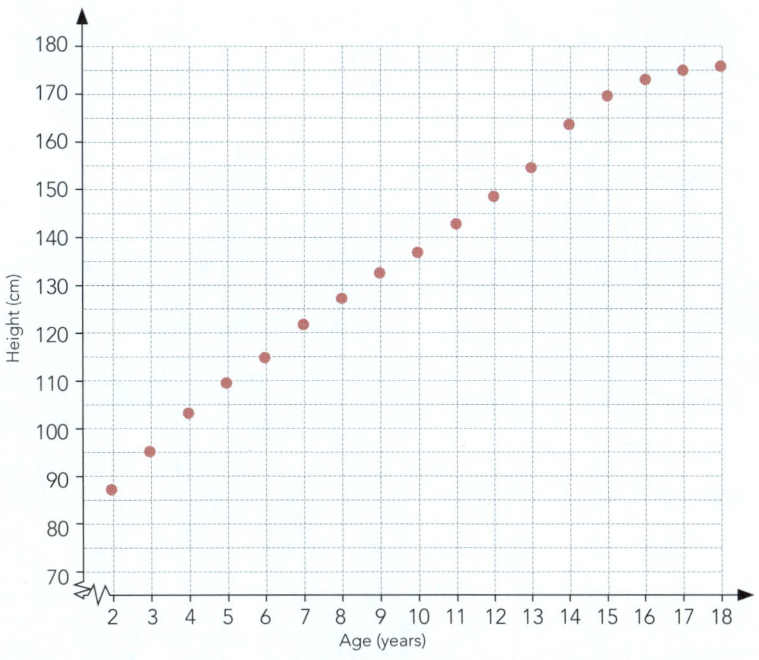

a When Toby started school when he was five, his height was 110 cm. ☐

b Toby grew by 25 cm between the ages of 13 and 17. ☐

c Toby grew more slowly when he was over 15 than when he was between 10 and 15. ☐

8 At the end of the camp, the 30 students wrote down their favourite activity.

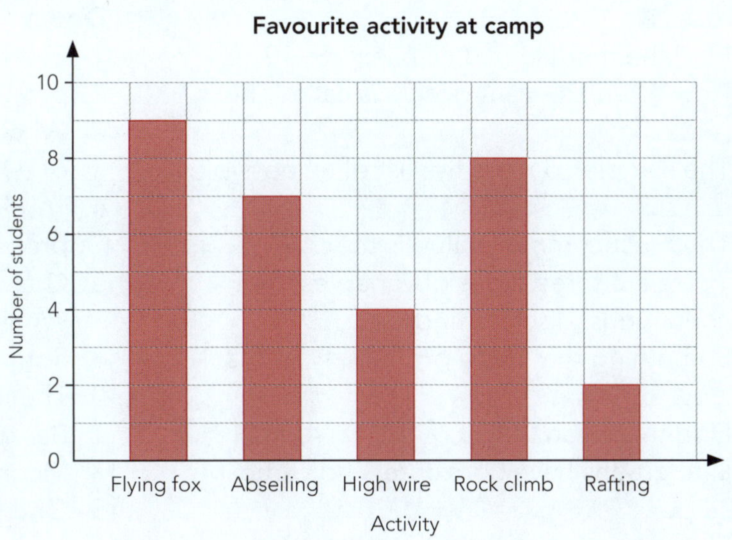

a The rock climb was the most popular activity and rafting was least popular. ☐

b The number of students who chose the high wire was double the number who chose rafting. ☐

c Exactly half the class wrote down either abseiling or the rock climb. ☐

ISBN: 9780170447256

Challenge 5

Any numerical answers will be written in word form, e.g. 7 = seven. Use the word bank at the bottom of the page if you are stuck.

Across

3 Find the median of 3, 5, 6, 6, 8, 9, 10.
6 How often an event occurs is called the ______.
9 The sample space is the list of all possible ______?
12 The most common value is the ______.
14 There are three types of variables: continuous, discrete and ______.
18 Something that has a probability of 1 is ______.
19 Find the mean of 5, 3, 9, 10, 15, 4, 7, 11.
21 Line graphs have horizontal and vertical ______.
22 Find the range of 5, 6, 2, 9, 12, 14, 8, 5, 6.
23 We often use experiments to get ______ of probabilities.

Down

1 Events that are more likely have ______ probabilities than unlikely events.
2 What tool can we use to find the probabilities of two events? Probability ______.
4 You find an arrow in the middle of this circular probability tool.
5 Graphs with pictures are known as ______.
7 What do you call more than one die?
8 Something that has a probability of 0 is ______.
10 The middle number is known as the ______.
11 Bar graphs can be vertical or ______.
13 Means are sometimes known as ______.
15 One measure of spread is the ______.
16 The mode of 9, 5, 7, 3, 1, 5, 0, 4, 7, 4, 8, 9, 5.
17 A ______ graph is a circular graph.
20 The side of a coin that is not heads is ______.

bigger	averages	axes	descriptive	pie	certain
eight	range	spinner	six	median	five
outcome	mode	impossible	pictographs	trees	tails
frequency	dice	horizontal	twelve	estimates	

 ISBN: 9780170447256

Revision 1

1 Select the best term to complete the sentence.

is certain to	is very likely to	is likely to	is unlikely to	won't

An event has a probability of 0.3, so it ____________________ occur.

2 Write the shaded proportion as:

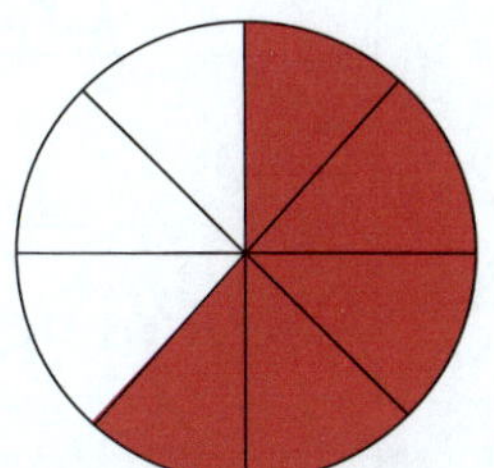

a a fraction. ____________

b a decimal. ____________

c a percentage. ____________

3 Convert these probabilities into decimals and state which is more likely.

$\frac{1}{5}$ = ________ $\frac{3}{16}$ = ________ More likely: ________

4 Consider the bag of marbles. What is the probability of pulling out:

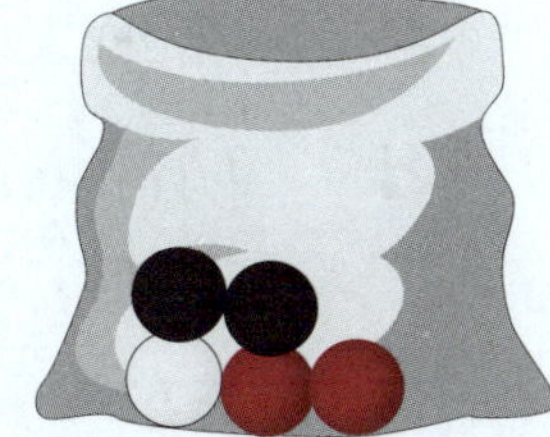

a a black marble? ____________

b a red or white marble? ____________

c a blue marble? ____________

5 A coin is tossed and then the spinner is spun.

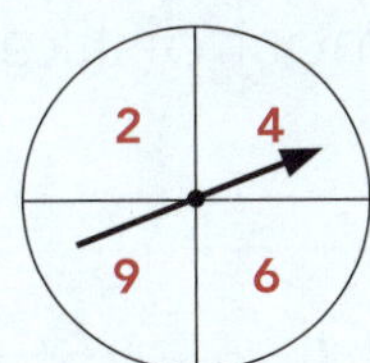

	2	4	6	9
H				
T		T4		

a Complete the table.

b How many outcomes are there? ____________

c What is the probability of getting heads and then a 6? ____________

d What is the probability of getting an odd number? ____________

e How many 9s would you expect to get if you spun the spinner 100 times? ____________

ISBN: 9780170447256

6 Complete the sentence with the best term: descriptive/discrete/continuous.

Favourite activity at camp is an example of a ________________ variable.

7 This graph is a pictograph/bar graph/line graph. (Circle best term.)

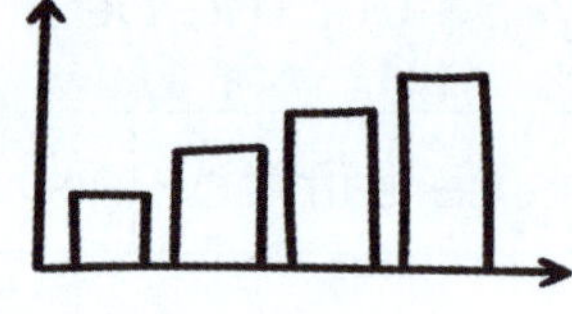

8 The 24 members of a class were asked which chore they most disliked.

Chore	Tally	Frequency
Dishes	|||	
Vacuuming	𝍸 𝍸 ||	
Cleaning bathrooms		9

a Complete the table.

b What fraction of the class disliked doing dishes most?

c Show this data on the pie graph.

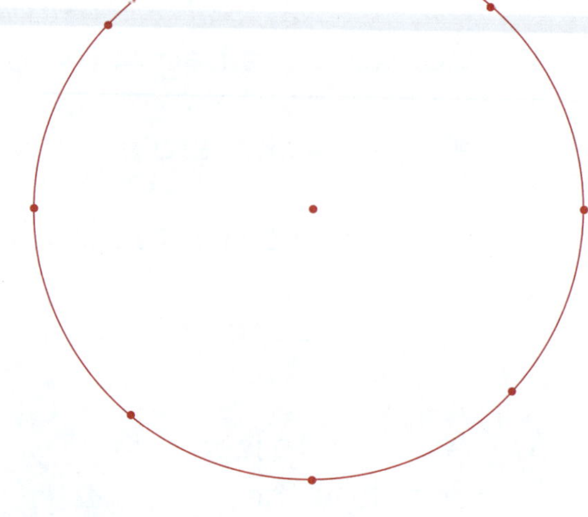

d What was the most unpopular chore?

____

e What is the probability that a member of the class most disliked cleaning bathrooms?

____

9 A group of friends are deciding what to do on teacher only day.

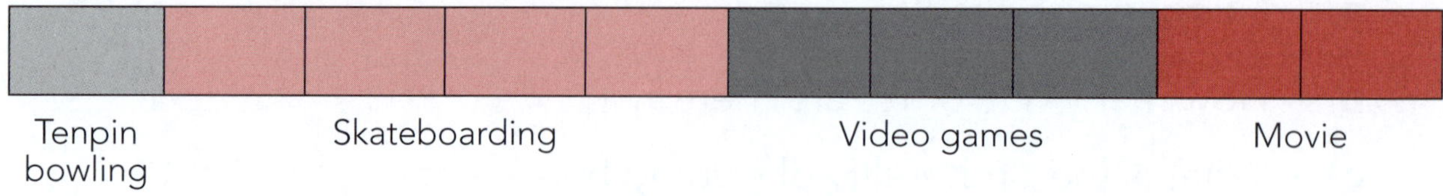

a What is the probability that a friend wanted to go skateboarding? ________________

b What is the probability that a friend didn't want to go skateboarding? ________________

 ISBN: 9780170447256

10 The graph shows the number of filled rolls sold by the canteen last week.

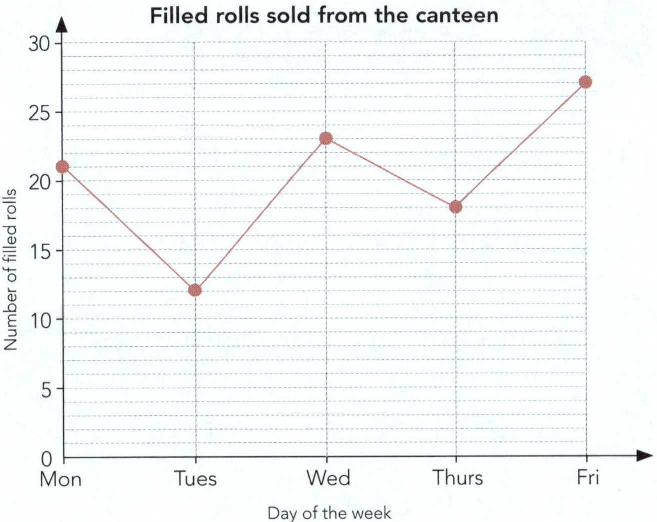

a What is the total number of filled rolls sold on Thursday and Friday? ____________

b More filled rolls sell on hot days. Which day do you think was the hottest? ____________

c Raj said that twice as many filled rolls sold on Wednesday compared to Tuesday.
Is he correct? ____________ Explain: ____________________

____

11 Ten students wrote down the number of bikes that were in each of their households.

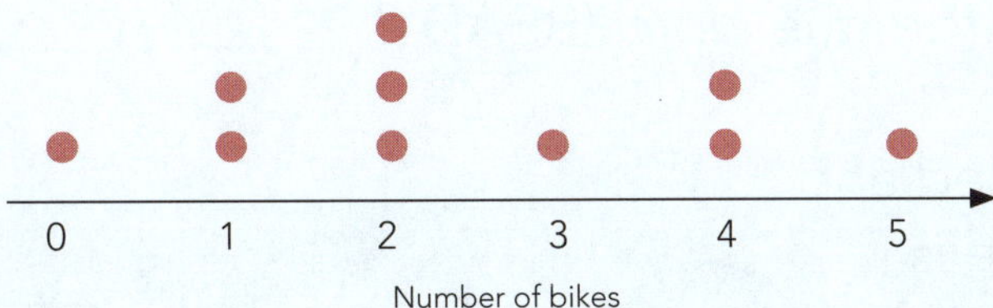

a Write this data as a list.

____

b Complete the following.

Mean = ______ Median = ______ Mode = ______ Range = ______

Put ticks or crosses in the boxes to indicate whether each is a correct interpretation or not.

c Most households had fewer than 2 bikes. ☐

d The most common number of bikes was 3. ☐

e Two households had 4 bikes each. ☐

ISBN: 9780170447256

Revision 2

1 Select the best term to complete the sentence.

is certain to	is very likely to	is likely to	is unlikely to	won't

An event has a probability of 0.9, so it ______________________ occur.

2 Write the shaded proportion as:

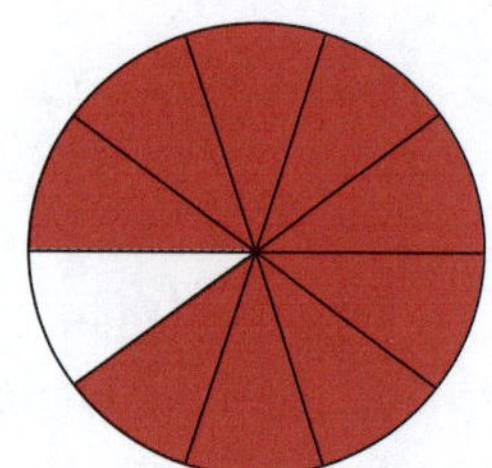

a a fraction. ______________

b a decimal. ______________

c a percentage. ______________

3 Convert these probabilities into decimals and state which is more likely.

84% = ________ $\frac{17}{20}$ = ________ More likely: ________

4 Consider the spinner. What is the probability of spinning:

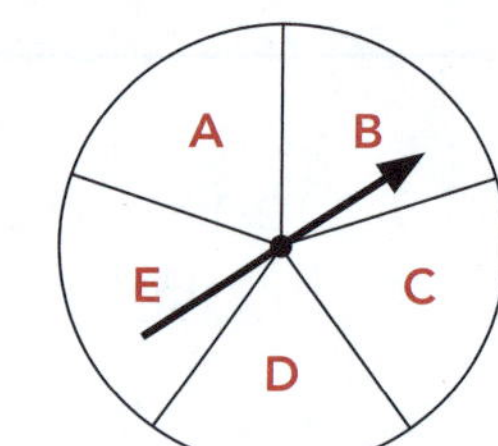

a the letter D? ______________

b a vowel? ______________

c a letter from the word 'BEAD'? ______________

5 A coin is tossed and then a marble is drawn out of the bag and then put back.

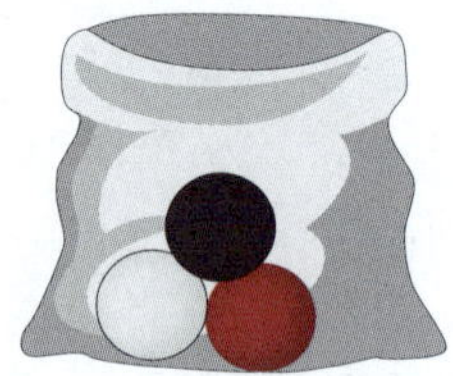

	Black	Red	White
H			HW
T			

a Complete the table.

b How many outcomes are there? ______________

c What is the probability of getting tails and a red marble? ______________

d What is the probability of getting heads and a red or a white marble? ______________

e How many red marbles would you expect to get if you drew a marble out of the bag and then replaced it 60 times? ______________

 ISBN: 9780170447256

6 Complete the sentence with the best term: descriptive/discrete/continuous.

My height is an example of a ________________ variable.

7 This is a pie graph/bar graph/pictograph. (Circle best term.)

8 Rawiri and his family went fishing. They caught 20 fish in total, including four gurnard.

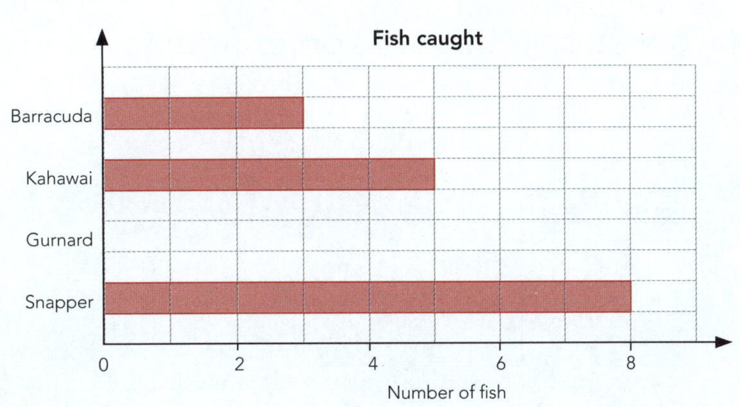

a Complete the bar graph.

b What percentage of the fish were snapper? ________________

c Most of the fish caught were snapper or barracuda. True/False

d Kahawai, gurnard and snapper are good to eat. Barracuda is not good to eat. If a fish is picked at random, what is the probability that it is not good to eat?

____

9 From the table, select the most appropriate value for each position on the scale. You will not need to use all the values.

25	36	53	58	43	28	20	48	38

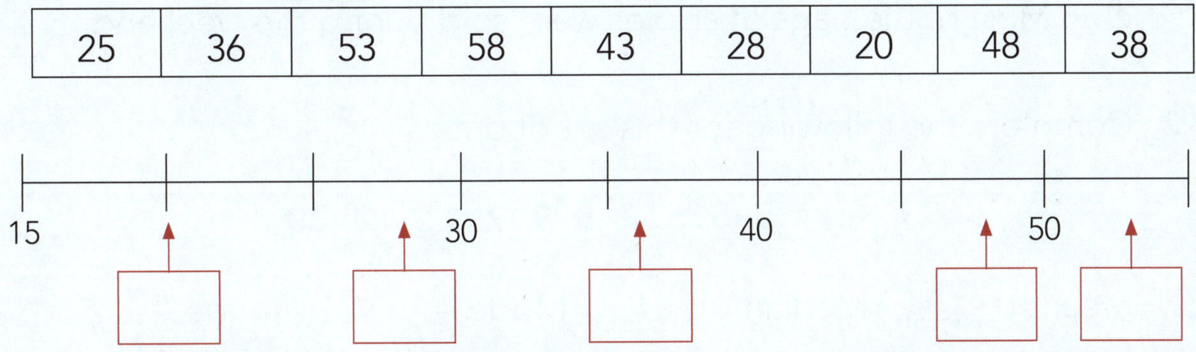

ISBN: 9780170447256

10 There were 24 items in the library returns box.

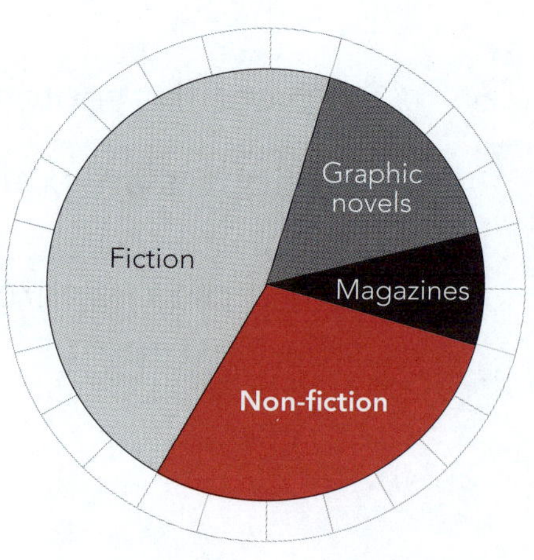

a 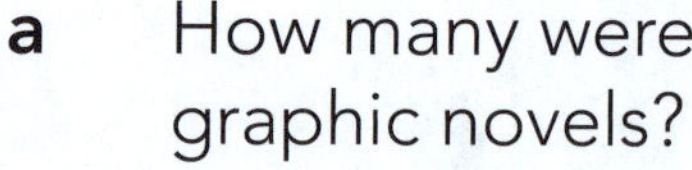
How many were graphic novels? ______________

b 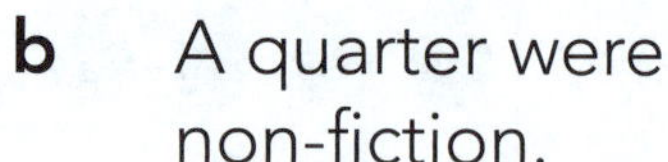
A quarter were non-fiction. True/False

c What is the probability that an item was either a magazine or a graphic novel? ______________

11 Tamati sells bags of apples from his roadside stall.

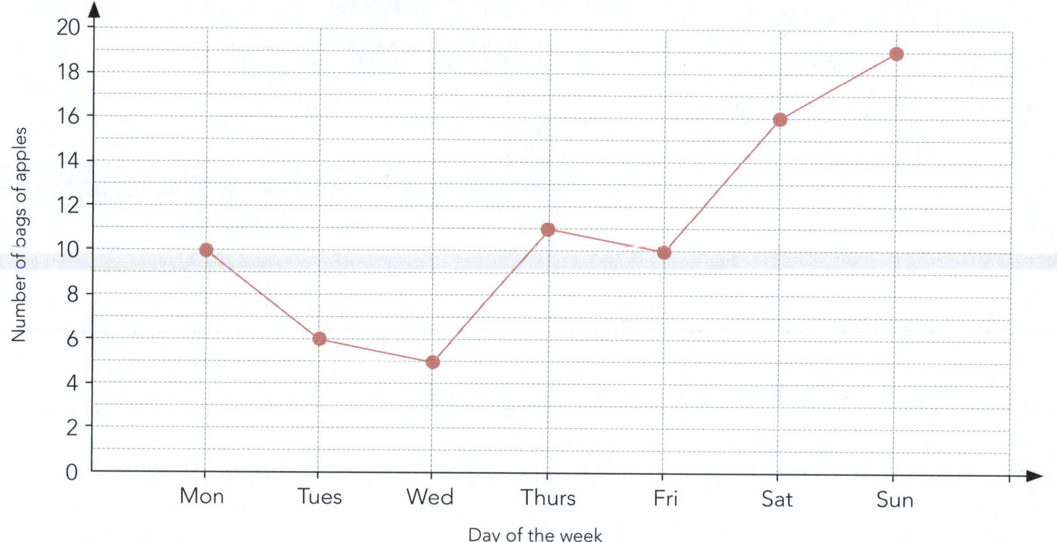

Put ticks or crosses in the boxes to indicate whether each is a correct interpretation or not.

a He sold five more bags on Thursday compared with Wednesday. ☐

b The mean number of bags of apples sold each day is 11. ☐

c Most of the bags of apples were sold during the weekend. ☐

12 Complete the following for this set of data:

5 5 5 7 8 9 9 11 12 30

Mean = ______ Median = ______ Mode = ______ Range = ______

ISBN: 9780170447256

Answers

Probability (pp. 6–28)

Useful language (pp. 6–7)

1

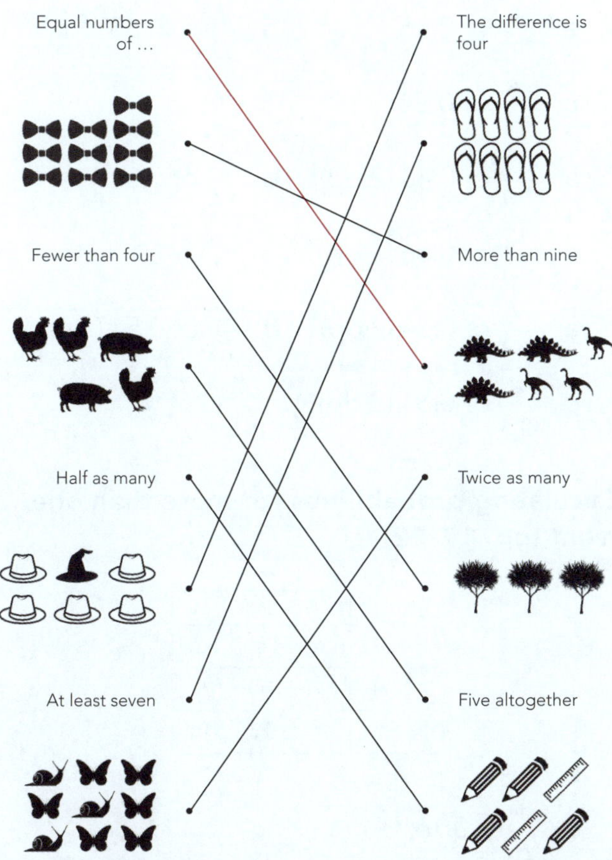

Words used to describe probabilities (p. 8)

1 a maybe; b almost certain; c probable; d guaranteed; e likely; f no way; g impossible

2 a likely; b certain; c impossible; d unlikely; e even chance

The probability scale (p. 9)

1 a sure thing
0.9 very likely
0.7 probable
0.5 even chance
0.3 maybe
0.1 slight chance
0 no chance

Using numbers to describe probabilities (pp. 10–11)

1

Shaded circle picture	Fraction	Decimal	Percentage
	$\frac{1}{10}$	0.1	10%
	$\frac{1}{5}$	0.2	20%
	$\frac{1}{4}$	0.25	25%
	$\frac{3}{10}$	0.3	30%
	$\frac{1}{3}$	$0.33\dot{3}$	$33.\dot{3}\%$
	$\frac{2}{5}$	0.4	40%
	$\frac{5}{10} = \frac{50}{100}$	0.5	50%
	$\frac{3}{5}$	0.6	60%
	$\frac{2}{3}$	$0.66\dot{6}$	$66.\dot{6}\%$
	$\frac{7}{10}$	0.7	70%
	$\frac{3}{4}$	0.75	75%
	$\frac{4}{5}$	0.8	80%
	$\frac{9}{10}$	0.9	90%

Calculating probabilities with one favourable outcome (pp. 13–15)

1 a $\frac{1}{2}$ or 0.5

2 a $\frac{1}{6}$ or $0.1\dot{6}$ b $\frac{1}{6}$ or $0.1\dot{6}$
c 0

3 a $\frac{1}{6}$ or $0.1\dot{6}$ b $\frac{2}{6}$ or $\frac{1}{3}$ or $0.\dot{3}$
c 0

4 a $\frac{1}{4}$ or 0.25 b $\frac{2}{4}$ or $\frac{1}{2}$ or 0.5
c 0

5 a $\frac{2}{5}$ or 0.4 b $\frac{3}{5}$ or 0.6
c 0

6

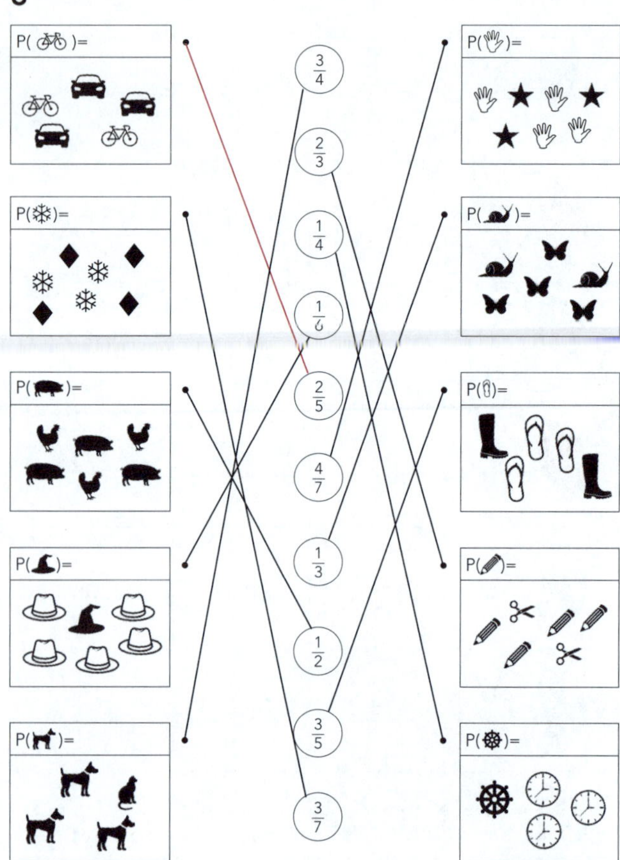

Calculating probabilities with more than one favourable outcome (pp. 16–18)

1 a $\frac{3}{5}$ or 0.6 b $\frac{4}{5}$ or 0.8
c 1

2 a $\frac{2}{6}$ or $\frac{1}{3}$ or $0.\dot{3}$ b $\frac{4}{6}$ or $\frac{2}{3}$ or $0.\dot{6}$
c $\frac{4}{6}$ or $\frac{2}{3}$ or $0.\dot{6}$ d $\frac{6}{6}$ or 1

3 a $\frac{5}{9}$ or $0.\dot{5}$ b $\frac{6}{9}$ or $\frac{2}{3}$ or $0.\dot{6}$
c $\frac{9}{9}$ or 1

4 a $\frac{2}{6}$ or $\frac{1}{3}$ or $0.\dot{3}$ b $\frac{3}{6}$ or $\frac{1}{2}$ or 0.5
c $\frac{3}{6}$ or $\frac{1}{2}$ or 0.5 d $\frac{5}{6}$ or $0.8\dot{3}$
e $\frac{2}{6}$ or $\frac{1}{3}$ or $0.\dot{3}$

5 a $\frac{3}{10}$ or 0.3 b $\frac{5}{10}$ or $\frac{1}{2}$ or 0.5
c $\frac{7}{10}$ or 0.7

6 a $\frac{4}{11}$ or $0.\dot{3}\dot{6}$ b $\frac{7}{11}$ or $0.\dot{6}\dot{3}$
c $\frac{6}{11}$ or $0.\dot{5}\dot{4}$

7 a $\frac{6}{14}$ or 0.43 (2 dp) b $\frac{7}{14}$ or 0.5
c $\frac{12}{14}$ or 0.86 (2 dp)

8 a $\frac{7}{13}$ or 0.54 (2 dp) b $\frac{7}{13}$ or 0.54 (2 dp)
c $\frac{4}{13}$ or 0.31 (2 dp)

Calculating probabilities for more than one event (pp. 19–22)

1 a

		Spinner		
		A	B	C
Coin	H	HA	HB	HC
	T	TA	TB	TC

b 6

c $\frac{1}{6}$ or $0.1\dot{6}$

d $\frac{2}{6}$ or $\frac{1}{3}$ or $0.\dot{3}$

2 a

		Die					
		1	2	3	4	5	6
Coin	H	H1	H2	H3	H4	H5	H6
	T	T1	T2	T3	T4	T5	T6

b 12

c $\frac{1}{12}$ or $0.08\dot{3}$

d 2

e $\frac{6}{12}$ or $\frac{1}{2}$ or 0.5

ISBN: 9780170447256

3 a

Event one (coin)	Event two (spinner)	Outcomes
H	X	HX
	Y	HY
	Z	HZ
T	X	TX
	Y	TY
	Z	TZ

b 6

c $\frac{1}{6}$ or $0.1\dot{6}$

d 2

4 a

	Silver	Gold
Red	RS	RG
Green	GS	GG

b 4

c $\frac{1}{4}$ or 0.25

d $\frac{2}{4}$ or $\frac{1}{2}$ or 0.5

5 a

Event one	Event two	Outcomes
Coffee	Scone	Coffee, Scone
	Donut	Coffee, Donut
Tea	Scone	Tea, Scone
	Donut	Tea, Donut

b 4 **c** 2

6 a

		Shirt		
		Yellow	**Red**	**White**
Shorts	**Black**	BY	BR	BW
	Grey	GY	GR	GW

b Black and grey

c 6

d $\frac{2}{6}$ or $\frac{1}{3}$ or $0.\dot{3}$

e $\frac{2}{6}$ or $\frac{1}{3}$ or $0.\dot{3}$

Probability experiments (pp. 23–24)

1 a

	Number	Probability	
Heads	120	$\frac{120}{250}$	0.48
Tails	130	$\frac{130}{250}$	0.52
Total	250		1

b No. Because only 250 tosses were done. In order to be certain you would need to do a lot more tosses.

c No. Because what has happened in the past does not change the probability of tossing a head.

d 500

2 a Once **b** Twice

c More

d No. Because what has happened in the past does not change the probability of not rolling a four.

e 100

3 a 2 **b** 1

c Fewer **d** 100

Comparing decimals (p. 25)

1 a 0.93 **b** 0.73

c 0.58 **d** 0.91

e 0.76 **f** 0.47

2

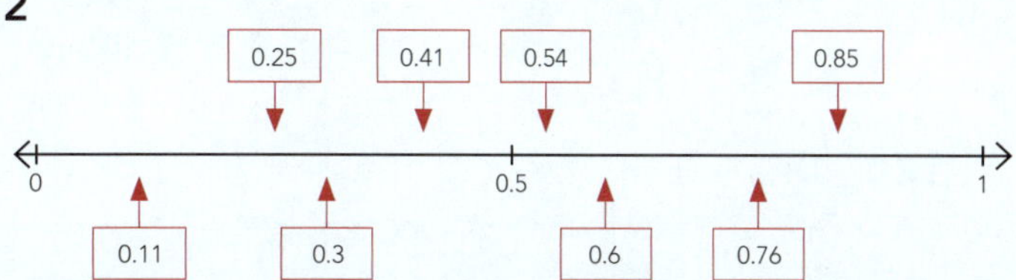

Comparing probabilities (pp. 26–27)

1 $\frac{1}{4} = 0.25$ $0.3 = 0.3$

More likely: 0.3

2 85% = 0.85 0.82 = 0.82

More likely: 85%

3 25% = 0.25 $\frac{1}{3} = 0.3\dot{3}$

More likely: $\frac{1}{3}$

4 0.5 = 0.5 $\frac{2}{5} = 0.4$

More likely: 0.5

ISBN: 9780170447256

5 $\frac{9}{10} = 0.9$ $92\% = 0.92$

More likely: 92%

6 $61\% = 0.61$ $0.6 = 0.6$

More likely: 61%

7 $\frac{4}{5} = 0.8$ $\frac{2}{3} = 0.6\dot{6}$

More likely: $\frac{4}{5}$

8 $\frac{1}{3} = 0.3\dot{3}$ $30\% = 0.3$

More likely: $\frac{1}{3}$

9 $\frac{1}{9} = 0.1\dot{1}$ $10\% = 0.1$

More likely: $\frac{1}{9}$

10 $\frac{11}{20} = 0.55$ $0.5 = 0.5$

More likely: $\frac{11}{20}$

11 $\frac{3}{5} = 0.6$

$0.59 = 0.59$

$61\% = 0.61$

0.59 Least likely | $\frac{3}{5}$ | 61% Most likely

12 $18\% = 0.18$

$\frac{1}{6} = 0.1\dot{6}$

$0.2 = 0.2$

$\frac{1}{3}$ Least likely | 18% | 0.2 Most likely

13 $33\% = 0.33$

$\frac{1}{3} = 0.3\dot{3}$

$0.34 = 0.34$

33% Least likely | $\frac{1}{3}$ | 0.34 Most likely

Challenge 1 (p. 28)

1 Spinner 2

Spinner 2 because the probability of landing on an A is 0.4, while the probability of getting an A using spinner 1 is just $0.\dot{3}$.

2 Bag A

Bag A because the probability of pulling out a red marble is 0.43, while the probability of getting red in bag B is just 0.4.

Statistical concepts (pp. 29–30)

Census and sample (p. 29)

	Question	Census or sample?	Why?
1	What is the New Zealand's favourite TV programme?	Sample	The outcome is not important.
2	Should New Zealand change its captial city?	Census	The outcome is very important.

Types of variables (p. 30)

1 Descriptive
2 Continuous
3 Discrete
4 Continuous
5 Discrete
6 Continuous
7 Discrete

Data display (pp. 31–65)

1

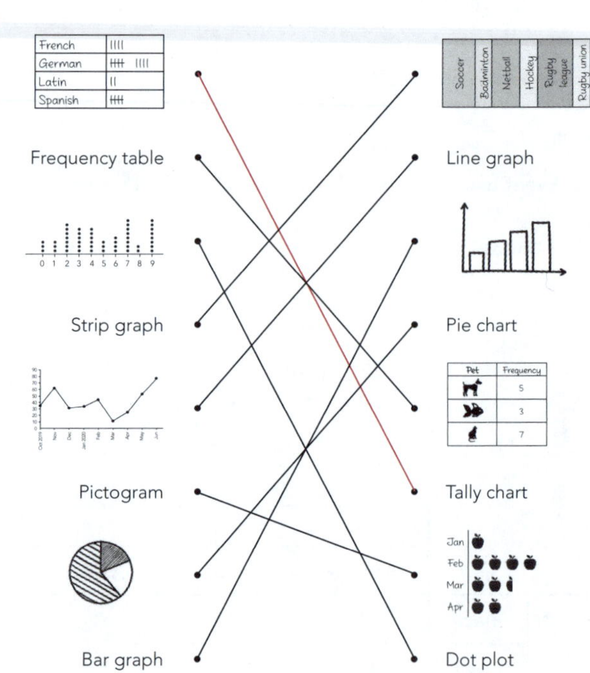

ISBN: 9780170447256

Tally charts and frequency tables (pp. 32–36)

1 a

Item	Tally	Frequency
Ice cream	𝍸 𝍸 |	11
Milkshake	𝍸 ||	7
Ice block	|||	3
Drink	||||	4

b Ice cream
c Ice block
d 14
e 14
f $\frac{4}{25} = 0.16$
g 0.72
h 44%

2 a

Item	Tally	Frequency
Football	𝍸	5
Rugby ball	𝍸 𝍸 |||	13
Basketball	𝍸 ||||	9

b 14
c Rugby
d 27

3 a

Item	Tally	Frequency
Pies	𝍸 𝍸 |	11
Filled rolls	𝍸 𝍸 𝍸 𝍸 |	21
Cream buns	𝍸 𝍸 𝍸 |||	18

b Filled rolls
c 50
d 42%

4 a Pear
b 3
c $\frac{5}{12}$

5 a

Item	Tally	Frequency
	|||	3
	𝍸 ||||	9
	||||	4
	𝍸 |||	7
	||	2
	Total	25

b Dog
c 24
d 12%

Pictographs (pp. 37–39)

1 a 3
b High heels
c 12

2 a Fly
b 5
c 10

3 a 2
b Car
c Bus

4

Subject	
English	♥ ♥
Science	♥ ♥ ♥
Mathematics	♥ ♥
Music	♥
Art	♥ ♥ ♥ ♥

Pie graphs (pp. 40–44)

1 a 9 students
b Peach
c Bananas, Grapes
d 28
e $\frac{6}{28}$ or $\frac{3}{14}$

2 a Pīwakawaka
b Tūī
c Riroriro
d 11
e 40%
f $\frac{5}{15}$ or $\frac{1}{3}$

3 a Black
b 3
c –10
d $\frac{12}{20}$ or $\frac{3}{5}$ or 0.6

4 a Mince and cheese
b Mince
c Steak
d 125
e $\frac{28}{125}$ or 0.224
f $\frac{50}{125}$ or 0.4

5

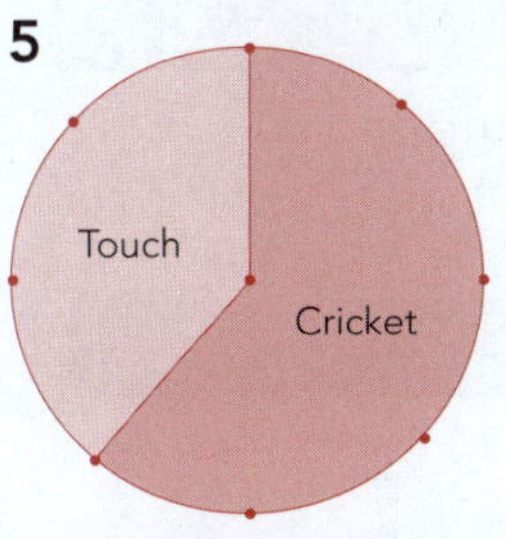

6

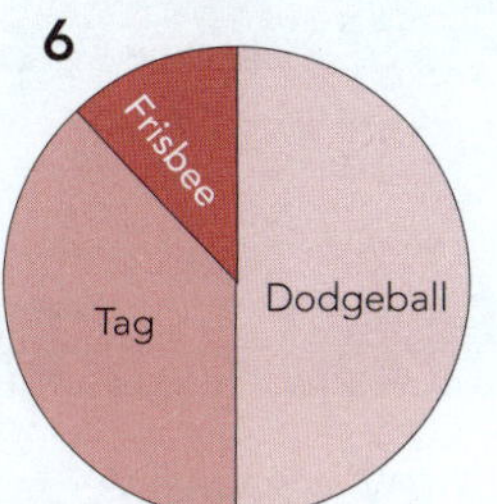

7 Your pie graph might look different. Check it with your teacher.

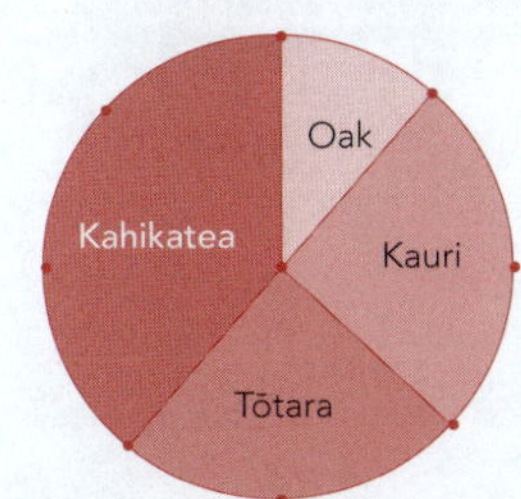

c $\frac{3}{8}$

ISBN: 9780170447256

Challenge 2 (p. 44)

a $\frac{80}{10} = 8$

b 16

c Dog

d 40

e $\frac{24}{80} = 0.3$

f 10%

g Disagree.
Sixteen students want a fish and 24 want a cat. Double 16 is 32, so for this statement to be true, 32 students would need to want a cat.

Strip graphs (pp. 45–47)

1 a Brussels sprouts
b Peas
c Beans and cauliflower

2 a 3
b Ponga
c 9
d $\frac{3}{9}$ or $\frac{1}{3}$

3 a July
b October
c 4
d 14

4 a 5
b 5
c $\frac{4}{12}$ or $\frac{1}{3}$
d 16

5

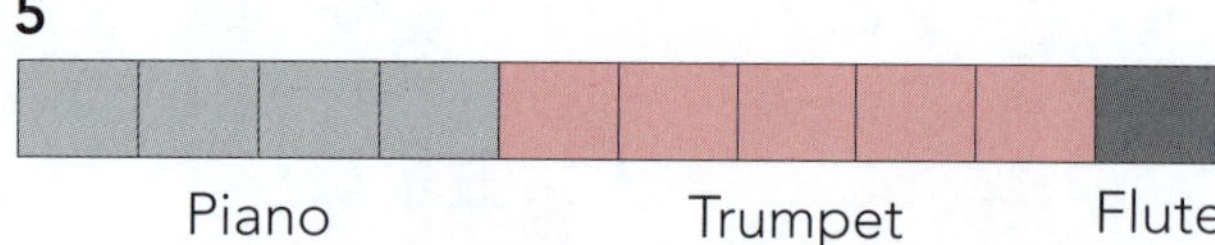

6

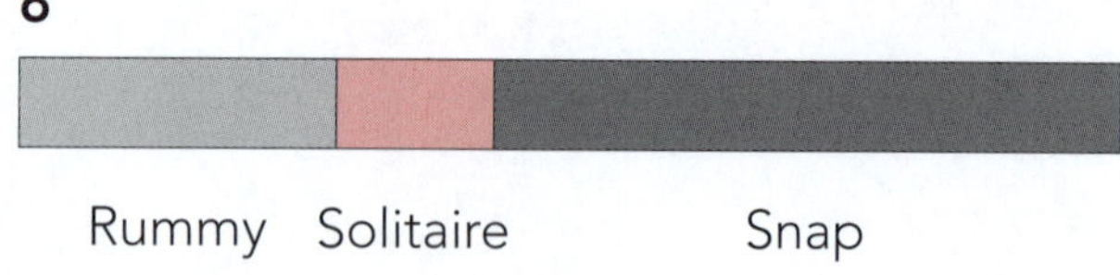

7

Reading axes (pp. 48–49)

1 Major 2 Minor 1 2 Major 5 Minor 1 3 Major 2 Minor 1 4 Major 10 Minor 5

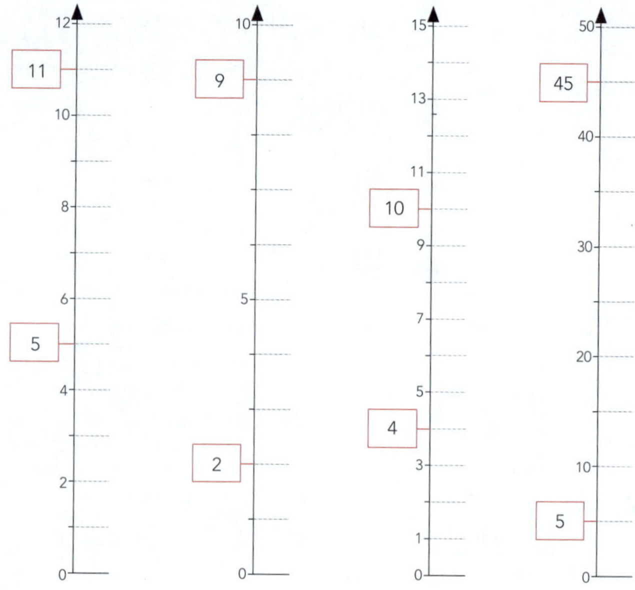

5 Major 2 Minor 1

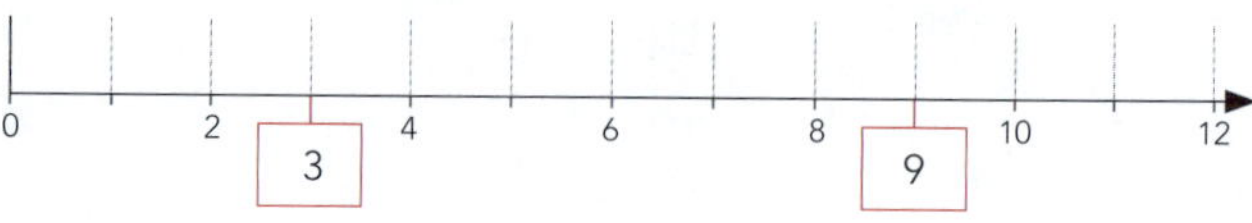

6 Major 5 Minor 1

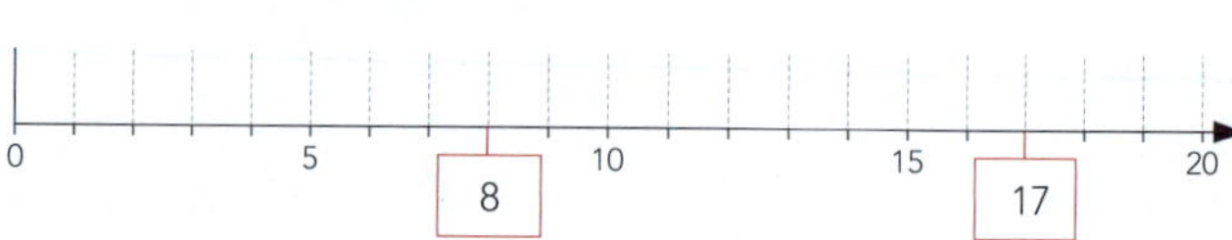

Bar graphs (pp. 50–54)

1 a 2
b Blue cod
c Snapper and kahawai
d 20

2 a Music items
b Magazines
c She borrowed twice as many music items as non-fiction books.

3 a 4
b Strongly agree
c 16
d $\frac{23}{43}$

4 a Tabby
b 25
c 40
d $\frac{15}{40}$ or $\frac{3}{8}$ or 0.375

ISBN: 9780170447256

5

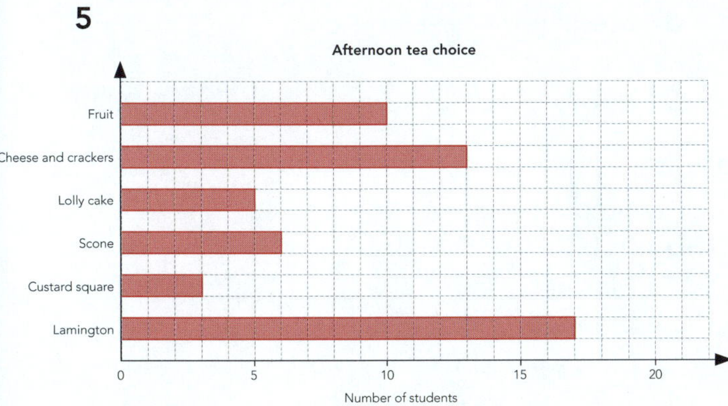

6

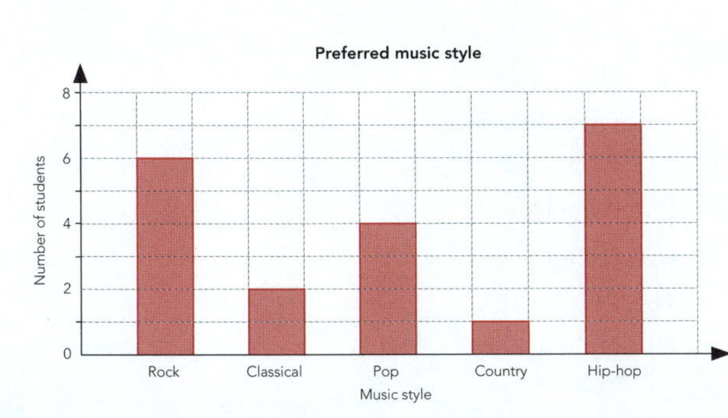

Challenge 3 (p. 54)

a 2
b 11
c Friday
d 16
e She didn't see any pīwakawaka on this day.
f Disagree.
On two days she saw more tūī.

Line graphs (pp. 55–58)

1 **a** Monday
b 15
c Tuesday and Friday
2 **a** 4
b May
c 1
3 **a** 51 minutes
b Week 5
c Week 4
d Because it took her longer to do the run than the day before.

4

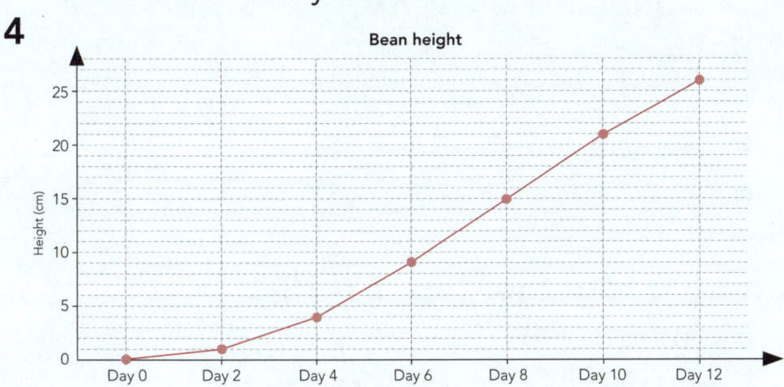

5

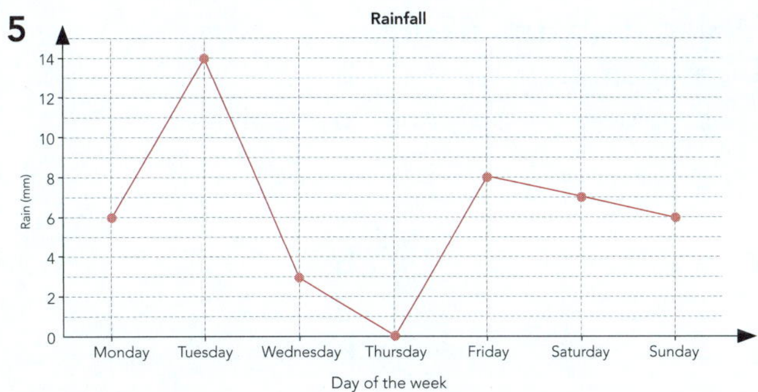

Challenge 4 (p. 58)

a 16
b Sunday
c Tuesday
d Wednesday
e Friday
f 246
g Disagree.
On Wednesday, there were more hot dogs sold than pies. However, overall it appears that generally pies are more popular.

Dot plots (pp. 59–61)

1 **a** 7 **b** 17
c 4
2 **a** 7 **b** 5
c 6 **d** $\frac{3}{26}$
3 **a** 5 **b** 5
c 8 **d** $\frac{9}{26}$ or 0.36

4

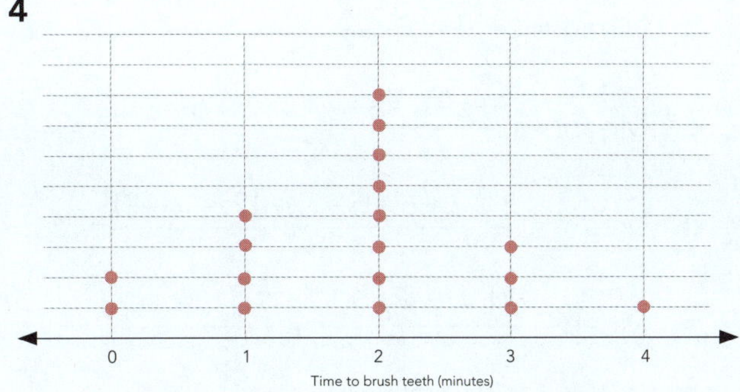

5

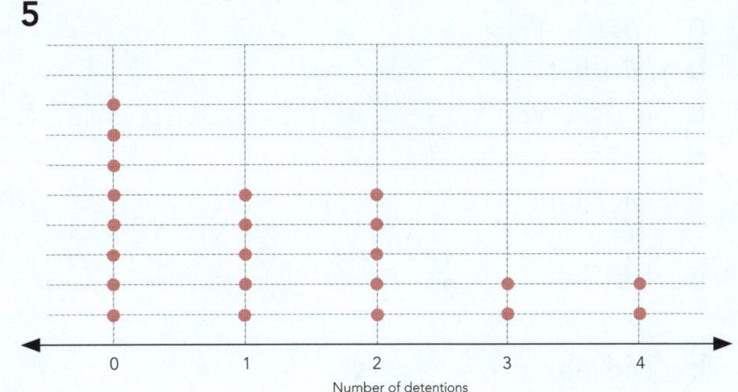

ISBN: 9780170447256

Mixing it up (pp. 62–65)

1 a Labrador b 6
c Pug d Collie
e $\frac{1}{3}$ or $0.\dot{3}$

2 a Beef b 4
c 15 d 20%

3 a 3 b 5
c 5 d $\frac{8}{26}$ or $\frac{4}{13}$

4 a Nectarines b 12
c Oranges d 9

5 a 3 b Chickens
c Ducks d 30

6 a 18 b 22
c 4 d 13

7 a 5 b Tidying room
c Laundry d 1
e $\frac{11}{49}$

8 a Cars b 5
c Cars were twice as likely to go past as bikes.
d 16 e 12.5%

Data analysis (pp. 66–75)

Measures of centre (averages) (pp. 66–71)

1 a Mean = $\frac{4+9+3+6+1+7}{6} = 5$

b Mean = $\frac{1+7+3+2+5+8+10+12}{8} = 6$

c Mean = $\frac{9+5+0+3+7+1+5+6+2+7}{10} = 4.5$

d Mean = $\frac{5+3+6+5+5+12+16+0}{8} = 6.5$

e Mean = $\frac{21+26+22+27+29+23}{6}$

$= 24.\dot{6}$ or 24.7 (1 dp)

2 a Median = 7
b Median = 6
c Median = 3
d Median = 5
e Median = 1

3 a Median = $\frac{6+8}{2} = 7$

b Median = $\frac{6+6}{2} = 6$

c Median = $\frac{8+12}{2} = 10$

d Median = $\frac{2+4}{2} = \frac{6}{2}$ or 3

e Median = $\frac{7+9}{2} = 8$

4 a 1 2 3 3 5 6 7 9
Median = 4
b 0 1 2 3 4 5 5 8 12 15
Median = 4.5
c 0 1 1 2 2 4 4 5 8
Median = 2
d 1 7 8 9 15 17 19 22
Median = 12
e 0 1 1 2 5 6 9 17 19
Median = 5

5 a Mode = 7
b Mode = 9
c Mode = 12
d No mode
e Modes = 2 and 8

6

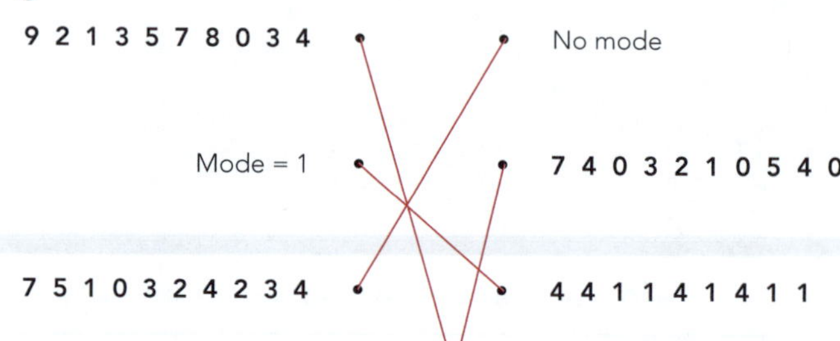

Mode = 0
Mode = 2

Measure of spread — range (p. 72)

1 a Range = 9 – 2 = 7
b Range = 14 – 3 = 11
c Range = 8 – 1 = 7
d Range = 20 – 10 = 10
e Range = 91 – 1 = 90
f Range = 101 – 16 = 85
g 6

Putting it together (pp. 73–75)

1 Mean = 6
Median = 7 Range = 11
Mode = 2 and 7

2 Mean = 7.875

 ISBN: 9780170447256

Median = 7.5 Range = 10
Mode = 5 and 11

3 0 1 2 2 4 5 6 7 9
Mean = 4
Median = 4 Range = 9
Mode = 2

4 1 3 4 5 6 8 9 11 12 18
Mean = 7.7
Median = 7 Range = 17
No mode

5 a 0 0 1 1 1 2 2 3 3 4
b Mean = 1.7
Median = 1.5 Range = 4
Mode = 1

6 a 1 1 2 3 3 3 3 4 4 4 5
b Mean = 3
Median = 3 Range = 4
Mode = 3

7 a 2 2 4 4 4 4 5 5 5 5 7 7
b Mean = 4.5
Median = 4.5 Range = 5
Mode = 4 and 5

8 a 0 0 0 0 0 1 1 1 2 2 3 4
b Mean = $1.1\dot{6} = 1.2$ (1 dp)
Median = 1 Range = 4
Mode = 0

9 a 0 1 1 1 1 1 1 2 2 2 2 2 2 2 3
b Mean = $1.5\dot{3} = 1.5$ (1 dp)
Median = 2 Range = 3
Mode = 0

Statistical literacy (pp. 76–79)

1 a × b ✓
c ×

2 a ✓ b ✓
c × d ×

3 a ✓ b ×
c ×

4 a × b ✓
c ✓ d ×

5 a × b ✓
c × d ✓

6 a × b ✓
c ✓

7 a × b ×
c ✓

8 a × b ✓
c ✓

Challenge 5 (p. 80)

							[1]B												
				[2]T		[3]S	I	X							[4]S				
				R			G		[5]P						P				
				E			G		I						I				
		[6]F	R	E	Q	U	E	N	C	Y		[7]D			N				
				S			R		T			I			N				
					[8]I				[9]O	U	T	C	O	M	E	S			
					M				G			E			R				
			[10]M		P		[11]H		R										
[12]M	O	D	E		O		O		A			[13]A							
			[14]D	E	S	C	R	I	P	T	I	V	E						
			I		S		I		H			E							
			A		I		Z		S			R		[15]R					
			N		B		O					A		A					
					L		N		[16]F			G		N				[17]P	
				[18]C	E	R	T	A	I	N		[19]E	I	G	H	[20]T		I	
							A		V			S		E		[21]A	X	E	S
				[22]T	W	E	L	V	E							I			
																L			
								[23]E	S	T	I	M	A	T	E	S			

Revision 1 (pp. 81–83)

1 An event has a probability of 0.3, so it **is unlikely to** occur.

2 a $\frac{5}{8}$ b 0.625
c 62.5%

3 1 in 5 = 0.2 $\frac{3}{16} = 0.1875$
More likely: $\frac{1}{5}$

4 a $\frac{2}{5}$ or 0.5 b $\frac{3}{5}$ or 0.6
c 0

5 a

	2	4	6	9
H	H2	H4	H6	H9
T	T2	T4	T6	T9

b 8 c $\frac{1}{8}$ or 0.125

d $\frac{2}{8}$ or $\frac{1}{4}$ or 0.25 e 25

6 Favourite activity at camp is an example of a **descriptive** variable.

7 This graph is a **bar graph**.

8 a

Chore	Tally	Frequency
Dishes	|||	3
Vacuuming	𝍸 𝍸 ||	12
Cleaning bathrooms	𝍸 ||||	9

b $\frac{3}{24}$ or $\frac{1}{8}$

ISBN: 9780170447256

c

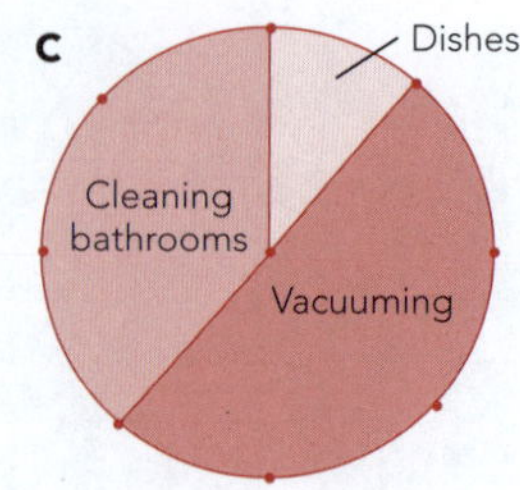

d Vacuuming

e $\frac{9}{24}$ or $\frac{3}{8}$ or 0.375

9 **a** $\frac{4}{10}$ or $\frac{2}{5}$ or 0.4 **b** $\frac{6}{10}$ or $\frac{3}{5}$ or 0.6

10 **a** 45

b Friday

c No. On Tuesday, 12 filled rolls were sold, and on Wednesday, 23 filled rolls were sold, not 24.
Or
Yes. Statistically, 12 is close to half of 24.

11 **a** 0, 1, 1, 2, 2, 2, 3, 4, 4, 5

b Mean = 2.4
Median = 2 Mode = 2
Range = 5

c ✗

d ✗

e ✓

Revision 2 (pp. 84–86)

1 An event has a probability of 0.9, so it **is very likely to** occur.

2 **a** $\frac{9}{10}$ **b** 0.9

c 90%

3 84% = 0.84 $\frac{17}{20} = 0.85$

More likely: $\frac{17}{20}$

4 **a** $\frac{1}{5}$ or 0.2 **b** $\frac{2}{5}$ or 0.4

c $\frac{4}{5}$ or 0.8

5 **a**

	Black	Red	White
H	HB	HR	HW
T	TB	TR	TW

b 6 **c** $\frac{1}{6}$ or $0.1\dot{6}$

d $\frac{2}{6}$ or $\frac{1}{3}$ or $0.3\dot{3}$ **e** 20

6 My height is an example of a **continuous** variable.

7 This graph is a **pictograph**.

8 **a**

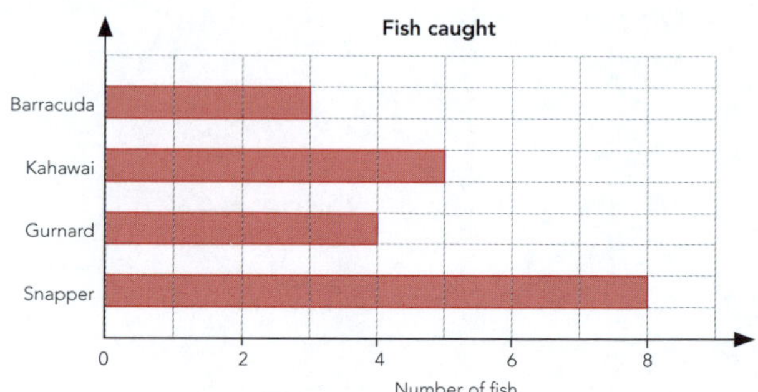

b 40%

c True

d $\frac{5 + 4 + 8}{20} = \frac{17}{20}$ or 0.85

9

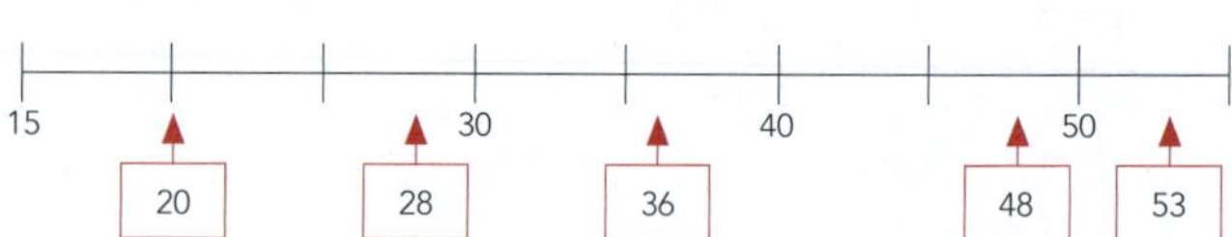

10 **a** 4

b False

c $\frac{2 + 4}{24} = \frac{6}{24}$ or $\frac{1}{4}$ or 0.25

11 **a** ✓

b ✓

c ✗

12 Mean = 10.1 Median = 8.5
Mode = 5 Range = 25

 ISBN: 9780170447256